Deaf Republic

by Dead Centre
& Zoë McWhinney

adapted from the book by
Ilya Kaminsky

SAMUEL FRENCH

FOR AMATEUR PRODUCTION ENQUIRIES

UNITED KINGDOM AND WORLD
EXCLUDING NORTH AMERICA
licensing@concordtheatricals.co.uk
020-7054-7298

Each title is subject to availability from Concord Theatricals,
depending upon country of performance.

USE OF COPYRIGHTED MUSIC

USE OF COPYRIGHTED THIRD-PARTY MATERIALS

IMPORTANT BILLING AND CREDIT REQUIREMENTS

NOTE

This edition reflects a rehearsal draft of the script and may differ from the final production.

DEAD CENTRE AND ROYAL COURT THEATRE IN ASSOCIATION WITH
DUBLIN THEATRE FESTIVAL AND COMPLICITÉ PRESENT

Deaf Republic

By Dead Centre and Zoë McWhinney
Adapted from the book by Ilya Kaminsky

Deaf Republic was first performed at the Royal Court Jerwood
Theatre Downstairs on Friday 29 August 2025 and subsequently at
the Dublin Theatre Festival on Thursday 2 October 2025.

Deaf Republic

By Dead Centre and Zoë Mcwhinney
Adapted from the book by Ilya Kaminsky

Cast (in alphabetical order)

Romel Belcher
Caoimhe Coburn Gray
Derbhle Crotty
Kate Finegan
Eoin Gleeson
Lisa Kelly
Dylan Tonge

Writer & Director **Bush Moukarzel**
Writer & Director **Ben Kidd**
Writer **Zoë McWhinney**
ISL Consultant and Translator (Dublin Theatre Festival) **Senan Dunne**
Set Designer **Jeremy Herbert**
Costume Designer **Mae Leahy**
Lighting Designer **Azusa Ono**
Video Director **Grant Gee**
Composer & Sound Designer **Kevin Gleeson**
Associate Sound Designer **Fred DeFaye**
Dramaturgs **Lydia Gratis & Jess Latowicki**
Aerial Consultants **Chrissie Ardill & Kat Cooley**
Puppetry Consultant **Cillian O Donnachadha**
Assistant Director **Liam Rees**
Intimacy Coordinators **Roisin O'Donovan & Abigail Kessel**
Fight Choreographer **Ciaran O'Grady**
Production Manager **Gavin Kennedy**
Video Programmer **Michael Dunne**
Lighting Programmer & Relighter **Peter Bond**
Sound Programmer & Audio Engineer **Aidah Sama**
Stage Manager **Sibéal Ní Mhaoileoin**
Assistant Stage Manager **Ross Smith**
Aerial Crew **Merlin Stone, Jenny Tufts, Marie Williamson, Joe Garcia**
Wardrobe Assistant & Dresser (Dublin Theatre Festival) **Eimear Hussey**
Producer **Tilly Taylor**
Associate Producer **Lianne Quigley**

For the Royal Court, on this production:

Company Manager **Mica Taylor**
Stage Manager **Amber Chapell**
Stage Supervisor **Steve Evans**
Lighting Supervisors **Lucinda Plummer & Deanna Towli**
Lighting Operator **Daisy Simmons**
Dresser **Katie Pollard**
Senior Dramaturg **Gillian Greer**
Lead Producer **Hannah Lyall**
Executive Producer **Steven Atkinson**

A Dead Centre and Royal Court Theatre co-production, in association with Dublin Theatre Festival and Complicité. Funded by The Arts Council of Ireland/An Chomhairle Ealaíon with creative production support from field:arts and ZooCo. London performances supported by Culture Ireland.

Supported by the T.S. Eliot Foundation.

With thanks to all of our Sign Language Interpreters including: Vanessa O'Connell, Romy O'Callaghan, Ciara Flatley, Aoife Harrington, Ela Cichocka, Leah Murray, Kristina Cregan, Aoife McLaughlin, Bernadette Ferguson, Catherine White, Ben Bridger, Deborah McLeod, Melissa Johnson, Heather Martin, Sue Barry, Luke Holdsworth, Louise Mitcham, Sophie Gunn, Natasha Trantom, Jadeaana Odle, Taz Hockaday, Bev Wilson, Bernadette Travers, Jemima Hoadley.

The Royal Court, Dead Centre and Stage Management wish to thank the following for their help with this production: SignKid, Daryl Jackson, Shane O'Reilly, Fiona Keller, Stephen Dodd, Barry O Donovan, Laura Rainsford, Chloe Commins, Isabel O'Grady, Rob Peate, The Wylie Agency, ArtFX, Tim Dollimore at The Media Workshop, Adam Fitzsimons / Connacht Production Services, Eugenia Genunchi, Anika Kidd, Seán Kenny, QLX, Anne Marie Jones, Isa Barrett.

Bush Moukarzel (Writer & Director)

Bush is co-artistic director of Dead Centre.

As co-writer and co-director, theatre for Dead Centre includes: **The Education of Rudolf Steiner (Schauspiel Stuttgart); Illness as Metaphor, LIPPY (Dublin Fringe); The World is Everything That is the Case, The Interpretation of Dreams (Burgtheater, Vienna); Chekhov's First Play, Hamnet, Beckett's Room, To Be a Machine (Version 1.0), Good Sex, To Be a Machine (Version 2.0) (Dublin Theatre Festival).**

Opera for Dead Centre includes: **Il Teorema di Pasolini, LASH (Deutsche Oper, Berlin); Bählaams Fest (Ruhrtriennale).**

As actor, theatre includes: **Returning to Reims (Manchester International Festival/ Schaubühne, Berlin/St Ann's Warehouse, New York).**

Ben Kidd (Writer & Director)

Ben is co-artistic director of Dead Centre.

As co-writer and co-director, theatre for Dead Centre includes: **The Education of Rudolf Steiner (Schauspiel Stuttgart); Illness as Metaphor, LIPPY (Dublin Fringe); The World is Everything That is the Case, The Interpretation of Dreams (Burgtheater, Vienna); Chekhov's First Play, Hamnet, Beckett's Room, To Be a Machine (Version 1.0), Good Sex, To Be a Machine (Version 2.0) (Dublin Theatre Festival).**

Opera for Dead Centre includes: **Il Teorema di Pasolini, LASH (Deutsche Oper, Berlin); Die dunkle Seites des Mondes (Staatsoper Hamburg); Bählaams Fest (Ruhrtriennale).**

As director, other theatre includes: **In the Night Time (Before the Sun Rises) (Gate), Spring Awakening (Headlong), The Shawl (Young Vic).**

Zoë McWhinney (Writer)

As actor, theatre includes: **Anthony and Cleopatra (Globe); Fisherman's Friend (Cre8 Theatre); Can Bears Ski (& Pied Piper Theatre), Everyday (Deafinitely Theatre); Lilies on the Land (Apollo Theatre Company); Red (Polka); Jack O'Kent (D-live!); The Two Fridas (Chickenshed/ Handprint).**

As BSL director, theatre includes: **Julius Caesar (Icarus Theatre Collective).**

As BSL consultant, theatre includes: **Generation 20, The Messenger (RSC/ Coventry City of Culture Trust).**

As BSL translator and visual vernacular consultant, theatre includes: **Rise of the Refrain (ZooCo).**

Chrissie Ardill (Aerial Consultant)

Chrissie Ardill is a professional performer, choreographer and aerial rigger.

Dance and aerial includes: Scarabeus Aerial Dance Theatre, Paperdoll Militia, All or Nothing Aerial Dance Theatre, Fidget Feet Aerial Dance Theatre, Full Tilt Aerial Theatre, Plan B Creative.

Choreography, movement direction and aerial/stunt consultancy includes: Helen Milne Productions, Theatre Gu Leor, Frozen Charlotte Theatre, Plan B Creative, Underhand Dance, Stuart Alexander.

Rigging includes: Diana Salles, Marc Brew Company, Hikapee Aerial Theatre, Skylarks Entertainment, All or Nothing Aerial Dance Theatre, Fidget Feet Aerial Dance Theatre.

Teaching and facilitation includes: Irish Aerial Dance Festival, European Aerial Dance Festival, National Theatre of Scotland, Aerial Edge, Edinburgh International Festival, Irish Aerial Creation Centre.

Romel Belcher (Performer)

Theatre includes: FAME Visukalen (& tour), Knockout, A Doll's House (Riksteatern Crea); The Sense Experiment (Vargkattens Production).

Television includes: Melodifestivalen, Sexy Hands, When the World Collides.

Peter Bond
(Lighting Programmer & Relighter)

As associate lighting designer, theatre and dance includes: WAKE (THISISPOPBABY/tour), MOSH (Dublin Fringe Festival/tour).

As relighter, dance includes: Carmen, Nutcracker Sweeties, Bold Moves [& chief LX] (Ballet Ireland); Night Dances, Birdboy (United Fall).

Caoimhe Coburn Gray (Performer)

Theatre includes: To Be a Machine (Version 2.0) (Dead Centre), Two Hundred Deer to Every Lion (bluehouse), The Race (Ark), Absent the Wrong (Once Off), Horse Ape Bird (Irish National Opera), Love+ (Malaprop/tour).

Television includes: Conversations with Friends, Valhalla.

Film inclues: Flicker.

Kat Cooley (Aerial Consultant)

Kat Cooley is a professional dancer, aerialist, choreographer and consultant.

Aerial and circus includes: Associate Artist (Fidget Feet Aerial Dance); All or Nothing, Gravity and Levity, Battle Royal, White Gold (Iron Oxide/Cuerda Producciones); Paradise Lost? (Scarabeus Aerial Dance Theatre).

Dance and movement includes: Les Commandos Percu, C-scape Dance Company, Commonwealth Handover Ceremony (Delhi), Attik Dance, Cantabile 2, Ringo Starr Concert (ECHO Arena).

Consulting includes: Zog (Freckle Productions), Motionhouse (Lumin), TearAway (Cie Breaked).

Teaching includes: European Aerial Dance Festival, Irish Aerial Dance Festival, Rise Youth Dance Company, DanceBase.

Amber Chapell (Stage Manager)

Theatre includes: **Antony & Cleopatra, The Duchess of Malfi (Globe); The Real and Imagined History of the Elephant Man (Nottingham Playhouse); Bloody Elle- A Gig Musical (SOHO/Traverse/Royal Exchange); Happy Meal (Australian tour/Brixton House); No Pay? No Way!, Let The Right One In, NORA: A Dolls House, The Almighty Sometimes, The Skriker, Yen, Hamlet (Royal Exchange); Counting Down to Christmas, Down the Rabbit Hole, Second Star to the Right (MAST); The Climbers (Theatre By The Lake); Oliver Twist, Sunshine on Leith, The Graduate, Sweeney Todd (Leeds Playhouse); Deep Blue Sea (Chichester); Pavilion, Uncle Vanya (Theatr Clwyd); The Da Vinci Code, Frankenstein, Little Shop of Horrors (Salisbury Playhouse); Troilus and Cressida (RSC); Rita Sue and Bob Too (tour).**

Derbhle Crotty (Performer)

For the Royal Court: **The Alice Trilogy, The Weir, Portia Coughlan (& Abbey).**

Other theatre includes: **The Brightening Air (Old Vic); Playboy Of The Western World, Summerfolk, The Merchant Of Venice (National); Hecuba, I'll Be The Devil, Macbeth, Macbett, Hamlet (& West End), Little Eyolf (RSC); The Beauty Queen Of Leenane (Young Vic); Richard III (Headlong); The Events, Crave/Illusions (Actor's Touring Company); An Ideal Husband, The Three Sisters, Sive (& Druid), The Dead, Marble, The Great Hunger, Anna Karenina, The Well Of Saints, The Mai, Katie Roche, Bailegangaire (Abbey); The Cherry Orchard, DruidShakespeare, The Silver Tassie, The Good Father, The Gigli Concert (Druid); The Approach (Landmark); Afterplay, Juno And The Paycock, The Home Place, Dancing At Lughnasa (Gate, Dublin); The Seagull, Everyday, Dubliners (Corn Exchange).**

Television includes: **Mayfair Witches, Small Town-Big Story, Vanishing Triangle, Come Home, Hidden Assets, Paula.**

Film includes: **To The Lighthouse, Mandrake, The Bright Side, Rosie, Citizen Lane, Noble, Stella Days, Joy, Notes On A Scandal, The Merchant Of Venice, Whalefall, Earmark.**

Awards include: **Irish Times Theatre Award for Best Actress (The Three Sisters), Irish Times Theatre Award for Best Actress (DruidShakespeare), Ian Charleson Award (Little Eyolf).**

Other: **Associate Artist at Abbey Theatre and RSC, member of the Druid Ensemble.**

Fred DeFaye
(Associate Sound Designer)

Fred DeFaye began his career has a recording and mixing engineer, including as the personal engineer for the Eurythmics on their albums Savage and Revenge, later working with artists such as Depeche Mode, Tom Petty, The Prodigy, Bob Dylan and Paddy Casey.

As sound designer, theatre includes: **The Gates of Kyiv (& Royal Windsor), Au Bord (& Triennale Milano), The Black Diamond (& Punchdrunk), People show 119: Ghost Sonata (People Show); Krapp's Last Tape [associate sound designer] (Barbican).**

As composer, dance includes: **Time/Dropper (Jose Agudo); Tree (Sweetshop Revolution); Pull Me Closer, Rush 1/2, Alone Together (LEVYdance).**

As sound designer & sound engineer, dance includes: **Strange Blooms, Material Men redux, Bayadère – The Ninth Life, Translocations [& sound editor], Material Men, Counterpoint [& sound consultant] (Shobana Jeyasingh/Sadlers); Enowate (Dickson MBI/Sadlers); Isadora Now (Viviana Durante/Barbican).**

As sound engineer, dance includes: **Portraits in Otherness, DUENDE (Akram Khan/Dickson MBI); Under Siege, Rite of Spring (Yang Liping); Dance for Ukraine (Ivan Putrov); Ten Thousand Tons of Moonlight, Nine Songs (Fengling).**

Michael Dunne
(Video Programmer)

Theatre includes: **Safe House (& Schaubühne/St. Ann's Warehouse), The Cave, The Sugar Wife (Abbey); The Jesus Trilogy (Project Arts Centre).**

Senan Dunne
(ISL Consultant and Translator)

Senan Dunne is a lecturer at the Centre for Deaf Studies at Trinity College Dublin and an accredited and registered Deaf interpreter. He has been passionately involved in Deaf theatre for over three decades, joining the Dublin Theatre of the Deaf in 1989. In the early 1990s, he was one of the original actors with Pan Pan Theatre, working closely with founder and director Gavin Quinn during the company's formative years.

Senan is passionate about Irish Sign Language, Deaf culture, and storytelling, and is committed to promoting Deaf visibility and inclusion across education, the arts, and public life.

Kate Finegan (Performer)

Theatre includes: **Dream Factory (Dublin Theatre Festival/Lords of Strut), Haus of Fash Hun (Dublin Fringe Festival/FemmeBizarre), The Wakefires (ANU Productions).**

Television includes: **The Walsh Sisters, Northern Lights, Fair City.**

Film includes: **Babaí Brain, Tarrac, Joyride.**

As writer, theatre includes: **Gammy (Project Arts Centre).**

Grant Gee (Video Director)

At the Royal Court: **Bluets.**

Other theatre includes: **Orlando (Schaubühne), The Silence (Götesborgs Stadsteater), The Cherry Orchard (Schauspielhaus), Sorry Beyond Dreams (Burgtheater), The Malady of Death (Barbican/Theatre des Bouffes du Nord).**

Opera includes: **The Blue Woman, New Dark Age (ROH); La Voix Humaine (Opéra National du Rhin).**

Film includes: **Bluebeards Castle [film director], Everybody Digs Bill Evans, The Gold Machine, Patience (After Sebald), Innocence of Memories, 8 Bit, PlacePrints, The True History of the 100 Mile City [director], Scott Walker: 30 Century Man [DOP and editor], Stones in Exile [DOP], Here For Life [editor].**

As director, television includes: **Bach St John Passion, Orchestra of the Age of Enlightenment, Meeting People is Easy.**

Awards include: **Outstanding Contribution in Documentary for International Filmmaker Festival New York (The Gold Machine), Best Documentary in Literature for Master of Art Film Festival Bulgaria (Innocence of Memories), Best Cinema Documentary Grierson Awards (Joy Division), Mojo Vision Award (Joy Division), Sound & Vision Award Best Music Film, CPH: Dox (Joy Division), Audience Award for Best Film at Gdansk (Joy Division), Audience Award for Best Film 'In-Edit' Barcelona (Joy Division), Sony Award (Zoo Radio).**

Eoin Gleeson (Performer)

Theatre includes: **A Midsummer Night's Dream (Turbine Theatre), FLYNN (Abbey).**

Television includes: **The Woman in the Wall, The Tourist.**

Kevin Gleeson (Composer & Sound Designer)

Theatre includes: **Krapp's Last Tape (Landmark/tour); Die Erziehung des Rudolph Steiner, Illness as Methaphor, Tystnaden, Alles, was der Fall ist, Katharsis, Die Traumdeutung Von Sigmund Freud, Chekhov's First Play, Shakespeare's Last Play, Beckett's Room, Hamnet, To Be a Machine (Version 1.0), Die Machine in Mir (Dead Centre/tour); The Pillowman, The Borrowers, Beginning, The Children (Gate, Dublin); Hammam, Pasolini's Salò Redubbed (Abbey); Invitation to a Journey (Galway International Arts Festival).**

Film includes: **Amanda, Mero, Nido, Duffle Bag Boy, The House Fell, Hard Rain, Amoeba.**

Lydia Gratis (Dramaturg)

Lydia Gratis is a multi-award winning organiser, consultant, cultural strategist and storyteller reshaping how racialised and marginalised Deaf communities are seen, included and centred across movements, media and systems. She is the Founder and Director of Saved By The Sign (SBTS), a Deaf-led social enterprise working at the intersection of racial justice, Deaf advocacy and systemic change through media, advocacy and education.

Teaching includes: **Council of Europe (Youth Department), Gallaudet University (Centre for Black Deaf Studies), European Union of the Deaf Youth (EUDY), Trinity College Dublin (Centre for Deaf Studies).**

Awards include: **Black and Irish Educator of the Year Award, Soirée Des Lumières Prix International, EUDY Honorary Member Award for Contribution to the European Deaf Community.**

Jeremy Herbert (Set Designer)

For the Royal Court: **4.48 Psychosis (& RSC), Cleansed, The Ugly One, Bliss, Alice Trilogy, Thyestes, Ashes and Sand, The Lights.**

Other theatre includes: **Elektra, This is Our Youth, Sexual Perversity in Chicago, Up For Grabs, Betrayal (West End); The Education of Rudolf Steiner (Schauspiel Stuttgart); The Silence (Stadsteater, Gothenburg); Hamlet, Blue Orange, The Glass Menagerie, Blackta (Young Vic).**

Music includes: **PJ Harvey Hope 6 Demolition Project (tour).**

Dance includes: **The Wind (Royal Ballet).**

Opera includes: **Die dunkle Seite Mondes, La Bianca Notte, Death in Venice (Hamburg State Opera); Rodelinda (ENO/Bolshoi); Man and boy DADA (Almeida); Mary of Egypt (Aldeburgh Festival).**

Art installations/performances include: **Underbelly (Frieze), Safe House (Young Vic), Derek Jarman: My Garden's Boundaries Are the Horizon (Garden Museum - UK Exhibition of the Year 2020).**

Awards include: **NESTA Dreamtime Fellowship, Barclay Best Design Award (4.48 Psychosis).**

Dylan Tonge Jones (Performer)

Theatre includes: **An Evening With Mere Mortals (& Smock Alley/Fringe), Waiting For Faro (& Civic/Moate) (The Viking); Alice and the Wolf (tour); The Rapture of Hugo Ball (Smock Alley); Birdy (Peacock); Grow (New Theatre).**

Lisa Kelly (Performer)

Theatre includes: **My Mother Said I Never Should (Fingersmiths).**

Film includes: **I See A Voice, The Letter, Remote Struttin', Reverberations Reload, Diagnonsense, Pole, Reverberations.**

Television includes: **Eastenders, Sex Education.**

Presenting includes: **Crafty Champions, Tiny Tunes.**

As BSL consultant, television and film includes: **Code of Silence, Aurora Orchestra, Silent Witness, The Boat Story, CBeebies Bedtime Stories.**

As director, theatre includes: **Nowhere To Escape, The Promise [associate director] (Deafinitely Theatre).**

As director, film includes: **Remember Me.**

Awards include: **Deaffest Best Film (Diagnonsense).**

Gavin Kennedy (Production Manager)

Theatre includes: **Illness as Metaphor, To Be a Machine (Version 2.0), Lippy, Good Sex, Beckett's Room (Dead Centre/tour); Everything Falls, Bellow (Brokentalkers/tour); Tarry Flynn, Danti-Dan (Livin' Dred/tour); Unspeakable Conversations (Once Off/tour).**

Jess Latowicki (Dramaturg)

Theatre includes: **Super Duper Close Up (Yard); Double Double Act (Unicorn); Tonight I'm Gonna Be The New Me (Soho); Gym Party, We Hope That You're Happy (Why Would We Lie?) (BAC); Get Stuff Break Free (National); Stationary Excess (Shunt).**

Film includes: **The Dream Factory.**

Mae Leahy (Costume Designer)

Theatre includes: **Illness as Metaphor (& Dublin Fringe Festival/Viernulvier), To Be A Machine (Version 2.0), Good Sex (Dead Centre); The Misanthrope (The Lir); Theatre for One 2025: Made in Cork, Theatre for One 2024 (& Cork Midsummer) (Landmark); Don't Copy Me (Gift Horse/ Samuel Beckett Theatre); Like We Were Born To Move (National Youth Theatre/ Abbey); Blue Thunder (Cathal Cleary & Kelly Phelan); Isla, Happy Birthday Dear Alice, Blackbird, The Beauty Queen of Leenane (Four Rivers); The Wandering Rocks (ANU); Dubliners (Corn Exchange); Blister (Síofra O'Mara & Sinéad Gallagher); Tess, Twelfth Night, War and Peace (Gift Horse); In Heat (Philomena Productions).**

Sibéal Ní Mhaoileoin (Stage Manager)

Theatre includes: **Illness as Metaphor (Dead Centre/tour); History Play, Exit, Pursued by a Bear (Dublin Theatre Festival); Men's Business (Finborough); Escaped Alone (Cork Midsummer Festival/ Project Arts Centre).**

Cillian O Donnachadha (Puppetry Consultant)

Theatre includes: **Beckett's Room (Dead Centre/Picollo Teatro), Polly Green Jeans (Talisman/tour), An Triail, The Gambler McCabe (Fíbín/tour).**

Television includes: **Simon Says, Gailearaí Scú Scú, Tír na nÓg, Bright Sparks.**

As actor, theatre includes: **Seachtopus (High Rock/tour); How To Catch a Star (Hullabaloo); The Shed (Carlow Arts Festival); Dáil100 (Dáil); Blessed/ Beannaithe (Smock-Alley); The Trial (Fíbín/ tour); A Christmas Carol, The Laramie Project (& Civic Theatre/The Helix) (About Face); My English Tongue My Irish Heart (Green Shoots/tour); Anglo the Musical (Bord Gais Energy); The Last Days of a Reluctant Tyrant (An Taibhdhearc); Caith Amach é (High Rock/tour); Antigone (Splódar/tour); The Year of the French (Heffron/tour); Lizzy Lavelle and the Vanishing (Aisling Ghear/tour); Michael Collins-The Musical (Cork Opera); Naked Will (Biscuits for Breakfast); Polly Green Jeans (Talisman/tour); La Cage Aux Folles (SFX).**

As actor, television includes: **Basú, The Crisis, Seacht, Glas Vegas, Ros na Rún, Incognito.**

As actor, film includes: **A Terrible Beauty, 20/22.**

Azusa Ono (Lighting Designer)

For the Royal Court: **Manhunt, Expendable.**

Other theatre includes: **East is South** (Hampstead); The Spy Who Came In From The Cold (West End/ Chichester Festival); A Mirror (& Almeida), Walden (West End); Grenfell in the words of survivors (National/ St. Ann's Warehouse); Romeo & Juliet (Royal Exchange); Macbeth (Shakespeare North/Lyric Hammersmith/ tour); Henry V (Sam Wanamaker/tour); Watch on the Rhine, A Doll's House, Part 2 (Donmar); Much Ado About Nothing (RSC); Can I Live?, Copyright Christmas, Smack That (& tour) (Barbican); Blue Orange, Concubine (Birmingham Rep); Lao Can Impression, Yvette (Southbank); Love Lies Bleeding (The Print Room); Thick As Thieves (Clean Break/tour); Abandon (Lyric); Effigies of Wickedness (Gate); Cuttin' It (Young Vic/tour); Darkness Darkness (Nottingham Playhouse); Peddling (New York 59E59/tour); We Are Proud...(Bush); The Love Song of Alfred J Hitchcock (Curve Leicester/tour).**

Opera includes: **The Magic Flute (Nevill Holt Festival Opera); Kairos Opera (V&A Museum).**

Other projects include: **COP27 Health Pavilion (Sharm El Sheikh); The Sleeping Tree (Brighton Dome); Aurora (Toxteth Water Reservoir Liverpool); Tate Live Exhibition – Joan Jonas (Tate).**

Liam Rees (Assistant Director)

As director, theatre includes: **5 Shorts (Young Vic), The Land That Never Was (Camden People's/tour), Sycamore Grove (Edinburgh Fringe), The Enlightened (HOME/Junges Ensemble Stuttgart), It's Criminal (Tron), The Devil Drinks Cava (A Play, A Pie, & A Pint).**

As associate director, theatre includes: **The Return of Danton (Theater an der Ruhr/ Münchner Kammerspiele).**

Aidah Sama (Sound Programmer & Audio Engineer)

Theatre includes: **The Second Woman (Cork Opera House); King Lear, The Borrowers [AV programmer] (Gate, Dublin); Somnium (Brú Theatre); Bellow (Broken Talkers); The Quare Fellow (Abbey); Polar Bear & Penguin (Paul Curley/tour); Unfortunate (Fat Rascal/tour).**

As in-house sound engineer at the Abbey, theatre includes: **An Old Song, Half Forgotten; Tales from the Holywell; Tartuffe; A Whistle in the Dark; Portia Coughlan; Bloody Sunday: Scenes from the Saville Inquiry; Rescue Annie; Walls and Windows; iGirl.**

Dance includes: **Scorched Earth, Volcano (Attic Projects/tour); Mám, Nobodaddy (Teac Damsa/tour); Impasse (Mufutau Yusuf/tour).**

Opera includes: **Elsewhere (Abbey).**

Ross Smith (Assistant Stage Manager)

Theatre includes: **Lovesong, Agreement (& Lyric), Piaf, Guest Host Stranger Ghost, Baby Groove, Gate Crashes Festival (Gate, Dublin); Krapps Last Tape (& Gaiety/ Adelaide Playhouse), Illness as Metaphor (& Dead Centre), Boyfriends (& tour), Listen a black woman is speaking, Hotel Happiness (Project Arts Centre); Feet Pics Aren't Free (Smock Alley); Of A Midnight Meeting (Bewely's Cafe Theatre); King Lear, Fantastic Mr. Fox, Othello, Cinderella (Mill); Distillation (IMMA).**

Opera includes: **Rigoletto, Salome (Bord Gais Energy); William Tell, Faust (Gaiety); L'Olimpiade (ROH/Le Theatre Equillbre, Switzerland/tour).**

Tilly Taylor (Producer)

Tilly is Producer at Dead Centre.

Theatre includes: **Illness as Metaphor, To Be a Machine (Version 2.0), Lippy (tour), Beckett's Room (tour) (Dead Centre); MOSH, You're Still Here, I Feel You Apart From Me, Trans Live Art Salon (Dublin Fringe Festival); Happy Days (Landmark Productions/Olympia Theatre).**

Dance includes: **Queen of the Meadows (Project Arts Centre); Dances Like a Bomb [associate producer] (Junk Ensemble/ tour); Glimmer (Live Collision International Festival).**

Film includes: **Heatsink, Learners.**

As assistant producer at Headlong: **Unprecedented (Century Films/BBC); Faustus: That Damned Woman (Lyric Hammersmith/Birmingham Rep); Europeans: Dramas from a Divided Union (Guardian); Acts of Resistance (Theatre Royal Plymouth/New Perspectives/ Brewery Arts Centre), Richard III (Bristol Old Vic).**

Lianne Quigley (Associate Producer)

Lianne Quigley is a Deaf artist and activist based in Ireland, working as a performer, director, writer and collaborating artist, often utilising Irish Sign Language (ISL) to express narratives and experiences. Lianne has worked with the Project Arts Centre to look at ways of expanding opportunities for Deaf artists and audiences; was one of the leaders for the campaign for the legal recognition of her language, Irish Sign Language, which was achieved in 2017; and she is also chairperson of the Irish Deaf Society, the Deaf-led civil rights organisation.

Theatre includes: **A Softer Kiss [writer/ performer] (Disrupt Disability Arts Festival), Possession [performer] (ART:2023), Beethoven 9th Symphony 'Ode to Joy' [performer](Cork Midsummer Festival and Homo Novus Festival, Latvia), Dear Ireland [writer/performer] (Abbey).**

Awards include: **Dublin Fringe Festival's Judges Choice Award (Deaf Translations Project).**

THE ROYAL COURT THEATRE

The Royal Court Theatre is the writers' theatre. It is a leading force in world theatre for cultivating and supporting writers - undiscovered, emerging and established.

Since 1956, we have commissioned and produced hundreds of writers, from John Osborne to Mohamed-Zain Dada. Royal Court plays from every decade are now performed on stages and taught in classrooms and universities across the globe.

Through the writers, the Royal Court is at the forefront of creating restless, alert, provocative theatre about now. We open our doors to the unheard voices and free thinkers that, through their writing, change our way of seeing.

We strive to create an environment in which differing voices and opinions can co-exist. In current times, it is becoming increasingly difficult for writers to write what they want or need to write without fear, and we will do everything we can to rise above a narrowing of viewpoints. Through all our work, we strive to inspire audiences and influence future writers with radical thinking and provocative discussion.

ROYAL COURT

X royalcourt f royalcourttheatre

Supported using public funding by
ARTS COUNCIL
ENGLAND

ARTS COUNCIL ENGLAND

DEAD CENTRE

Dead Centre is a theatre company based in Dublin led by artistic directors Ben Kidd and Bush Moukarzel, and producer Tilly Taylor.

Their projects include Illness as Metaphor (2024), Good Sex (2022), To Be a Machine (Version 1.0) (2020), Beckett's Room (2019), Hamnet (2017), Chekhov's First Play (2015) and LIPPY (2013).

They have also created new work at Schauspiel Stuttgart (The Education of Rudolf Steiner, 2024), Burgtheater, Vienna (The Interpretation of Dreams, 2020 and Alles, was der Fall ist, 2021), Göteborgs Stadsteater (The Silence, 2021), and Schaubühne, Berlin (Shakespeare's Last Play, 2018). They have directed opera at Deutsche Oper Berlin, Staatsoper Hamburg and Ruhrtriennale.

Their work has toured extensively around the world, including to Battersea Arts Centre, Young Vic, BAM, Dramaten, ITA, Théâtre de Liège, Hong Kong Festival, Brisbane Festival and Seoul Performing Arts Festival.

Formed in 2012 by Bush Moukarzel, Ben Kidd and Adam Welsh, Dead Centre are principally funded by the Arts Council of Ireland. Deaf Republic at Royal Court Theatre was made possible with the support of Culture Ireland.

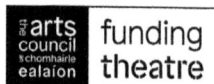

Cultúr Éireann
Culture Ireland
Promoting Irish Arts Worldwide for 20 years

arts council
an chomhairle ealaíon

funding theatre

ROYAL COURT SUPPORTERS

Our incredible community of supporters makes it possible for us to achieve our mission of nurturing and platforming writers at every stage of their careers. Our supporters are part of our essential fabric – they help to give us the freedom to take bigger and bolder risks in our work, develop and empower new voices, and create world-class theatre that challenges and disrupts the theatre ecology.

To all our supporters, thank you. You help us to write the future.

PUBLIC FUNDING

Supported using public funding by
ARTS COUNCIL ENGLAND

CORPORATE SPONSORS & SUPPORTERS

Aqua Financial Ltd
Cadogan
Character 7
Concord Theatricals
Edwardian Hotels, London
NJA Ltd. – Core Values & Creative Management
Nick Hern Books
Phone Locker
Riverstone Living
Sustainable Wine Solutions
Walpole

SISTER

CORPORATE MEMBERS

Bloomberg Philanthopies
Sloane Stanley

TRUSTS & FOUNDATIONS

Backstage Trust
Bruce Wake Charitable Trust
Chalk Cliff Trust
Clare McIntyre's Bursary
Cockayne - Grants for the Arts
The Common Humanity Arts Trust
Cowley Charitable Foundation
David Laing Foundation
The Davidson PlayGC Bursary
The Fenton Arts Trust
Foyle Foundation
Genesis Foundation
The Golsoncott Foundation
Jerwood Foundation
John Thaw Foundation
The Katie Bradford Arts Trust
The Lynne Gagliano Writers' Award
The Marlow Trust
Martin Bowley Charitable Trust
Molecule Theatre Ltd
The Noël Coward Foundation
Old Possum's Practical Trust
Richard Radcliffe Charitable Trust
The Royal Borough of Kensington & Chelsea Arts Grant
Rose Foundation
The Thistle Trust
The Thompson Family Charitable Trust
The T.S. Eliot Foundation
Unity Theatre Trust
Y.A.C.K F.O

INDIVIDUAL SUPPORTERS

Artistic Director's Circle

Eric Abraham
Katie Bradford
Jeremy & Becky Broome
Clyde Cooper
Debbie De Girolamo &
Ben Babcock
Dominique & Neal Gandhi
Lydia & Manfred Gorvy
David & Jean Grier
Charles Holloway OBE
Linda Keenan
Andrew Rodger and Ariana
Neumann
Jack Thorne & Rachel Mason
Sandra Treagus for
ATA Assoc. LTD
Sally Whitehill & Mark Gordon
Anonymous

Writers' Circle

Chris & Alison Cabot
Cas Donald
Robyn Durie
The Hon P N Gibson's Charity
Trust
Kater Gordon
Ellie & Roger Guy
Melanie J. Johnson
Nicola Kerr
Héloïse and Duncan
Matthews KC
Emma O'Donoghue
Clare Parsons & Tony Langham
Maureen & Tony Wheeler
Anonymous

Directors' Circle

Piers Butler
Fiona Clements
Professor John Collinge
Julian & Ana Garel-Jones
Carol Hall
Dr Timothy Hyde
Elizabeth O'Connor & Adam
Bandeen

Platinum Circle

Moira Andreae
Beverley Buckingham
Katie Bullivant
Anthony Burton CBE
Matthew Dean
Lucy & Spencer De Grey
Emily Fletcher
The Edwin Fox Foundation
Beverley Gee
Madeleine Hodgkin
Kate Howe
Roderick & Elizabeth Jack
Susanne Kapoor
David P Kaskel & Christopher
A Teano
Peter & Maria Kellner
Frances Lynn
Robert Ledger & Sally
Moulsdale
Mrs Janet Martin
Andrew McIver
Barbara Minto
Brian and Meredith Niles
Timothy Prager
Corinne Rooney
Sir Paul & Lady Ruddock
Sir William & Lady Russell
Anita Scott
Bhags Sharma
Dr Wendy Sigle
Rita Skinner
James and Victoria Tanner
Mrs Caroline Thomas
Yannis Vasatis
Ian, Victoria and Lucinda
Watson
Sir Robert & Lady Wilson

**With thanks to our Silver
and Gold Supporters, and
our Friends and Good
Friends, whose support we
greatly appreciate.**

Royal Court Theatre
Sloane Square,
London SW1W 8AS
Tel: 020 7565 5050
info@royalcourttheatre.com
www.royalcourttheatre.com

Artistic Director
David Byrne
Executive Director
Will Young
Artistic Director's Office
Manager
Natalie Dodd

Senior Associate
Playwright & Dramaturg
Gillian Greer
Associate Playwright
& Young Writers'
Associate
Beth Flintoff
Associate Playwrights
**Mike Bartlett,
Ryan Calais Cameron,
Vinay Patel, Ishy Din,
Nina Segal.**
Associate Artist (Art
Direction)
Guy J Sanders
New Plays Associate
Laetitia Somé
Resident Director
Aneesha Srinivasan
Artistic Co-ordinator
Ailsa Dann
Playwrights '73 bursary
attachment
Tife Kusoro

Head of Producing &
Partnerships
Steven Atkinson
Producer
Hannah Lyall
Casting Associate
Saffeya Shebli
New Writers &
Participation Producer
Tabitha Hayward
Producing Assistant
Hetty Opayinka

Director of
Development
Anuja Batra
Development Manager
Jen Lafferty
Development Officers
**Ellena Sychrava,
Nash Metaxas.**

Head of Production
Marius Rønning
Production Manager
Zara Drohan
Company Manager
Mica Taylor ^
Head of Lighting
Deanna Towli
Deputy Head of Lighting
Lucinda Plummer
Lighting Technician
Izzy Hobby
Lighting Programmer
Lizzie Skellett
Head of Stage
Steve Evans
Deputy Head of stage
Maddy Collins
Stage Show Technician
Oscar Sale
Head of Sound
David McSeveney
Deputy Head of Sound
Jet Sharp
Head of Costume
Lucy Walshaw

Director of Marketing &
Communications
Rachael Welsh
Marketing Manager
Benjamin McDonald
Digital Content
Producer (Videography)
Giovanni Edwards
Marketing Officer
Elizabeth Carpenter
Communications Officer
Natasha Ryszka-Onions
Press & Publicity
Bread and Butter PR

Finance Director
Helen Perryer
Finance Manager
Olivia Amory
Senior Finance &
Payroll Officer
Will Dry
Finance &
Administration
Assistant
Bukola Sonubi

Head of People
Olivia Shaw
People and Governance
Coordinator
Ayushi Mahajan

General Manager
Rachel Dudley
Front of House Manager
**Jennelle
Reece-Gardner**
Box Office Manager
Poppy Templeton
Senior Duty House
Manager
Ronay Poole
Ushers/Duty House
Managers
**Emer Halton-O'Mahony,
James Wilson.**
Box Office and Adminis-
tration Assistants
**William Byam Shaw,
Phoebe Coop,
Ollie Harrington, Aidan
Thompson-Coates.**
Stage Door Keepers
**James Graham,
Léa Jackson,
Paul Lovegrove.**

Head of Operations &
Sustainability
Robert Smael
Senior Bar & Floor
Supervisor
Lucy Stepan
Bar & Floor Supervisors
**Matthew Paul, Isa
Wood, Eleanor Willis.**
General Maintenance
Technician
David Brown

Thanks to all of our
Ushers and Bar staff.

^ The post of Company
Manager is supported
by Charles Holloway
OBE.

**ENGLISH STAGE
COMPANY**

Honorary Council
**Graham Devlin CBE
Martin Paisner CBE
Joyce Hytner OBE
Phyllida Lloyd CBE**

Council Chairman
Anthony Burton CBE

Members
**Jennette Arnold OBE
Noma Dumezweni
Neal Gandhi
Pamela Jikiemi
Mwenya Kawesha
Mark Ravenhill
Andrew Rodger
Anita Scott
Lord Stewart Wood**

Let's be friends. With benefits.

Our Friends and Good Friends are part of the fabric of the Royal Court. They help us to create world-class theatre, and in return they receive early access to our shows and a range of exclusive benefits.

Join today and become a part of our community.

Become a Friend (from £40 a year)

Benefits include:

- Priority Booking
- Advanced access to £15 Monday tickets
- 10% Bar & Kitchen discount (including Court in the Square)

Become a Good Friend (from £95 a year)

In addition to the Friend benefits, our Good Friends also receive:

- Five complimentary playtexts for Royal Court productions
- An invitation for two to step behind the scenes of the Royal Court Theatre at a special event

Our Good Friends' membership also includes a voluntary donation. This extra support goes directly towards supporting our work and future, both on and off stage.

To become a Friend or a Good Friend, or to find out more about the different ways in which you can get involved, visit our website: royalcourttheatre.com/support-us

The English Stage Company at the Royal Court Theatre is a registered charity (No. 231242)

FOREWORD

by Zoë Mcwhinney

I was born and raised Deaf, standing on the shoulders of multiple generations of Deaf and hearing sign language signers who migrated across Europe. Today I am a theatre creative, Visual Vernacular (VV) artist, British Sign Language (BSL) translator and Deaf culture consultant. This collaboration with Dead Centre feels particularly serendipitous given my personal and professional background, including an academic degree in International Relations. Deaf Republic's compelling themes of self-actualisation during occupation and war resonate deeply with me.

I was gifted Ilya's book before this project came to be. When I first read it, I was enchanted by the idea of a signed revolution and fictionally stretching the concept of "Deaf Gain", metaphorically using deafness as political leverage for resisting a violent oppression, as a way to sow fear and chaos in the narrow minds of oppressors.

The play, through the deaf character of Petya, explores the child-like fantasy of an entire town around a deaf child suddenly signing in solidarity – though tragically, post-mortem in Petya's case. This resonates deeply, considering that 90–95% of fellow deaf people are born into families with little to no prior exposure to sign language, deaf culture or deaf communities. Another sobering layer of Petya's killing is the reality that deaf people are genuinely being shot, or else subjected to excessive force for appearing to 'disobey' orders they could not hear nor understand by the people ignorant or fearful of them. Being raised within a signing community, let alone being born into a Deaf family is a privilege.

What's revolutionary about *Deaf Republic* for me is that it imagines a town of hearing people who take the initiative to plunge themselves into deafness and sign language as a means of resistance, and in turn they find pride and identity in it. Adapting the book into a play was an opportunity to flesh out the townspeople's individual journeys with acquiring sign language, and the new dynamics it creates amongst them.

Another element of the story that drew me in was how sign language intermingles with puppetry. The practice of injecting the soul into objects has echoes in sign language. For example, when a signer is recounting an event or a story, if you know the classifiers you'll notice that within the signed sentences, handshapes would move as if set within scenes, autonomous and alive in the eyes of the listeners and not merely someone else's fingers and limbs. Classifiers are like, you could say, puppets. A part of Visual Vernacular is an extension of this – expanding the art of giving consciousness into limbs, to a deeper detail and greater extent, often spontaneously to the delight of fellow folks, sitting or standing, typically in circles around a pub table, picnic mat or lounge room.

From the very beginning of this adaptation, d/Deaf artists and contributors have collaborated on the project, ensuring that both worlds are integrated equitably, so both d/Deaf and hearing audiences could receive and enjoy *Deaf Republic* on stage equally. The initial research and development phase with Dead Centre was in collaboration with SignKid, a Deaf hip-hop artist, Daryl Jackson, Shane O'Reilly and the Deaf dramaturg and activist Lydia Gratis. They explored the fascinating idea of subverting expectations around interpreting, flipping the concept of disability, accessibility and its stakeholders around, with actors Caoimhe Coburn Gray and Romel Belcher.

I joined Ben and Bush in the writer's room after these development phases, inheriting some early script and staging ideas from the team. Our discussions centered on how sign language would be represented in the adaptation, covering its grammar, history, and the art of storytelling through sign language.

One of the ways I began to create BSL poetry in the play was by finding and creating opportunities for continuous visual metaphors, encapsulated within signed dialogue between characters. Signed metaphors can create playful and powerful visual resonances that go beyond English words. For example, in the scene where Sonya and Alfonso are discussing their circumstances, the English script says "Where are we?" In sign language, to faithfully convey the intent of her line here, Sonya plucks at herself and Alfonso, and then pulls her hands into the air, rhetorically leaving them 'floating in limbo,' and then ends her signed question with the BSL sign for "WHERE?" When asked for clarification by Alfonso, the English script says "We are condemned to the present" – in sign Sonya goes back to the space where their imagined selves are floating, grabs them, bashing them onto the 'ground,' which is the same plane as the 'nowness, present, here' concept in BSL. In the English version, Alfonso responds saying "I'm honoured to be in the present with you." This is shown in sign by Alfonso creatively intermingling with Sonya's established hand positions by a soft closing of the fingertips whilst joining his hands together, like the BSL sign for "WITH", essentially conveying the same sentiment.

During the rehearsal process, we've been working with both Irish Sign Language (ISL) and BSL, on account of the show being performed at Royal Court Theatre in London, UK, and Dublin Theatre Festival, Ireland. It's noteworthy that while both aforementioned national languages derive partly from their Deaf communities' relationship with English, there are plenty of phrases and signs that aren't directly translatable between the different signed languages. The history of

British and Irish sign languages, and their international transmission and linguistic families, aren't concurrent with spoken English, despite the popular misconception that sign language exists in perfect parallel to spoken language.

If someone were to adapt the play into their native sign language, my number one advice would be to involve Deaf creatives from the start. And to those creatives, I advise you to treat the Sign Language as you would with any language, whether written or signed. The key is to consider the core direction and meaning of each scene, and how it could be best understood by your specific signing community and audience.

Sign language scripts are typically responsive to staging, because the signed sentences will be impacted by the direction and choices of tone and mood. Coincidentally, Dead Centre also usually works this way, discovering ideas in the writing process and then developing and changing these scripts in rehearsals, in response to the process and team. At the time of this publication, our sign language script is still in development, so this opening night edition of our playtext will feature the rehearsal draft of the English script and drawings demonstrating how the character's sign names are signed. These sign names were devised in rehearsals, based on the fingerspelt alphabet in Ukrainian Sign Language, a nod to Kaminsky's birthplace of Odessa – perhaps the spiritual blueprint for his invented town of Vasenka. The second edition of this publication will have a British Sign Language script, running concurrent with the final English one.

Zoë McWhinney
August 2025

CHARACTERS

SIGNER/ALFONSO
WORDER/SONYA
MOMMA GALYA – head of the Puppet theatre
KATE – one of Galya's puppeteers
LISA – one of Galya's puppeteers
PAVEL – one of the townspeople
SOLDIER

PUPPETS

PETYA – a deaf boy
ANUSHKA – child of Sonya and Alfonso

SETTING

Vasenka, a fictional town.

TIME

The present day.

CHARACTERS' SIGN NAMES

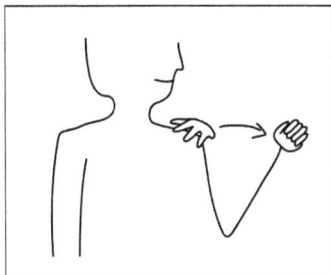

Hand starts on shoulder and pulls forward into a fist, which is like the Ukrainian sign for "A."

ALFONSO

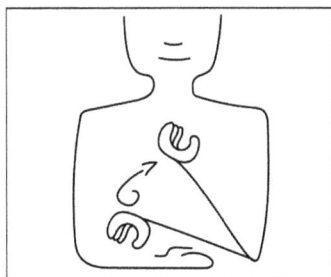

The hand, in a C shape, starts facing down on the opposite arm and then twists upwards. This hand shape is the Ukrainian sign for "C," which is the "S" sound in Ukrainian.

SONYA

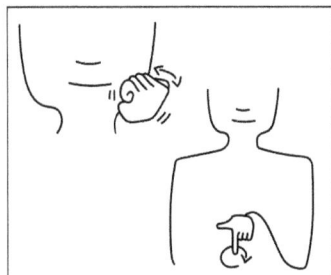

In a fist shape, the closed fingers tap the side of the chin for "Momma" – this is derived from the Ukrainian sign for grandma. Then the "G" hand shape in Ukrainian fingerspelling draws a small circle in the air, for "Galya."

MOMMA GALYA, head of the Puppet theatre

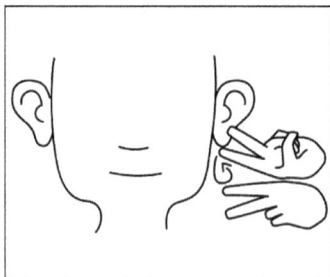

With the palm facing forwards, the top finger begins in front of the ear lobe. The fingers then draw a circle, as if following a hoop earring. This hand shape is the Ukrainian hand shape for "K."

KATE, one of Galya's puppeteers

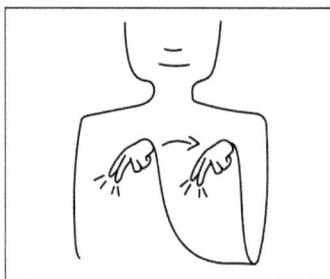

The two-fingered hand shape for the Ukrainian "L" travels from the far side of the chest to the near side, tapping the chest on both sides.

LISA, one of Galya's puppeteers

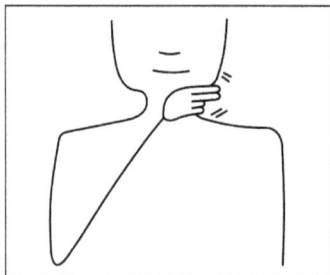

Two fingers wiggle, as if the fingers are a cigarette moving inside the mouth of someone talking. This hand shape is the Ukrainian sign for "P."

PAVEL, one of the townspeople

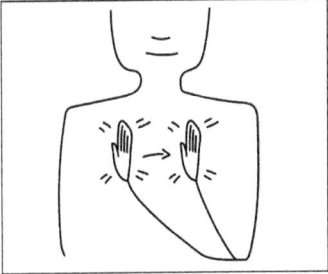

The thumb of the hand touches the chest and then jumps across and touches the chest a second time. This is the British Sign Language sign for "soldier."

SOLDIER

*(An empty stage. At the centre, we see a man. He is the **SIGNER**.)*

*(At the side of the stage, towards the front, where a sign-language interpreter might usually stand, we see a woman, she is the **WORDER**.)*

*(The **SIGNER** begins to sign. As he does so, the **WORDER** begins to speak.)*

SIGNER. *(Signs.)* Hello. Thank you for coming.

Before we start let me explain that tonight's show is an accessible performance which means words will be spoken out loud for those of you who are hearing.

I apologise in advance to the deaf audience members, and hope the person speaking over there doesn't become a distraction. I hope her words don't get in the way of the action.

In fact, if possible, I recommend you try to ignore her.

Just imagine she's not there.

But if anyone finds it hard to block her out, please remember, she's only there because I want this evening to be as accessible as possible.

(Captioned.) There might even be surtitles.

　　　(Pause.)

You see, I want everyone to understand everything.

After all, that's why we go to the theatre.

To try and understand each other.

To understand the world.

To make it accessible.

And the more accessible a story is, the better it will be understood.

Of course, what she says will only really be a *translation* of what I'm signing. An approximation. It's not easy to convey the full expressiveness of sign language in spoken English.

For example, if I make the sign for London.

> *(He does: a gesture conveying dizziness.)*

This sign communicates something about the experience of being in this city, how loud, disorientating and discombobulating it is.

Whereas, the word London, is rather more boring and neutral.

In a similar way, this is the sign for "colonialism"...

> *(The **SIGNER** reaches out, away from him, a grabbing motion.)*

...if you're white.

It suggests grabbing something, perhaps something that isn't yours.

But for Black signers the same sign is this:

> *(The **SIGNER** gestures towards herself, something being taken.)*

It suggests something being taken: your land, your language, your body, even.

You see, things get lost in translation.

So, tonight, it's entirely possible you'll only really know what's going on if you're deaf – I'm sure the interpreter will do her best to try and find the words.

(Pause.)

It's a strange job, when you think about it.

Interpreting.

Never speaking for yourself.

Just repeating whatever words I put into her mouth.

Kind of like a puppet.

(Pause.)

Let's see. What shall I make her say?

What if she was to say:

Hello.

My name is Sonya.

Let's try that.

> *(The* **SIGNER** *gestures for the* **WORDER** *to speak for herself.)*

WORDER. *(Unsigned, captioned.)* Hello.

My name is Sonya.

> *(Pause.)*

SIGNER. *(Signed, uncaptioned.)* Now of course that's not her real name.

I made it up.

But now she has a name, you care about her a bit more. You understand a bit more about who she is.

And the story is a little bit more accessible.

So, for tonight, even though we all know it isn't, for now, let's say her name is Sonya.

And let's say she's pregnant.

Really heavily pregnant.

And let's say her being pregnant might have something to do with her husband, Alfonso.

That's me.

Let's say I'm Alfonso.

And let's say I'm not actually deaf.

Well, I mean, *I* am, but let's say Alfonso isn't.

But it's easy enough to play a hearing character. All I have to do is rehearse my cues and remember to react whenever –

> *(A theatre light falls.* **ALFONSO** *looks around.)*

– I hear a loud sound.

> *(Pause.)*

So, yeah, I'm Alfonso and that's Sonya and we're married.

We're very much in love.

I love you, Alfonso.

I love you too, Sonya. But let's talk about that later. We have a story to tell.

Oh yes. Sorry.

Where should I begin?

I suppose you could start by telling them about our puppet theatre.

Good idea.

> *(Puppeteers –* **LISA** *and* **KATE** *– enter with a puppet theatre, watched over by* **MOMMA GALYA**. **PAVEL** *places a camera facing the puppet theatre.)*

(Signs.) Every weekend Sonya and Alfonso put on a puppet show in the town square.

Let's say this stage is the town square.

More specifically, let's say this is the town square in Vasenka.

There isn't really a place called Vasenka. I made it up.

Like Sonya, it's a fiction.

But I gave it a name to make it more accessible.

And a town is not a town without its people.

That's where you come in.

Let's say you're the townspeople of Vasenka.

Of course, I know you're not.

None of this happened to you

None of this happened to us – thank God.

We lived happily during the war.

But for now, even though you're not, let's say you're the townspeople of Vasenka.

And let's say you've all gathered in the town square to watch our puppet show.

Now, okay, you might be wondering why you've come to watch a puppet show – after all, puppet shows tend to be for children.

But even adults feel the need to gather together.

You see, even in troubled times, people need a little theatre.

God knows what we've all been through.

How much we've endured, here in Vasenka.

So tonight, in spite of everything that's happening, we can allow ourselves some light entertainment.

(*A gauze lowers over the stage. It is semi-transparent: allowing us to see a projected image and the stage at the same time.*)

(*On the gauze we see a live-camera projection of the puppet theatre.*)

(*Piano music plays.*)

(*Onstage, a puppet is lowered into the puppet theatre. It appears large on the screen.*)

(*It is a* **PUPPET OF ALFONSO**.)

(*Another puppet arrives. It is a* **PUPPET OF SONYA**, *holding a microphone.*)

(*She walks forward, turns to* **PUPPET-ALFONSO**, *and raises her microphone.*)

(**PUPPET-ALFONSO** *signs.*)

PUPPET-ALFONSO. (*Signed, captioned.*) Hello. Thank you for coming.

(**PUPPET-ALFONSO** *then turns to* **PUPPET-SONYA** *and points at her.*)

(*Captioned.*) And thank *you* for coming.

(*They walk towards each other and kiss.*)

(*They fall to the ground.*)

(*They have sex.*)

(**PUPPET-SONYA** *gets up.*)

PUPPET-SONYA. (*Captioned.*) Thank *you* for coming.

(**PUPPET-SONYA** *raises up out of view.*)

(**ALFONSO**'s hand appears in the puppet theatre and places a cigarette in the hand of **PUPPET-ALFONSO**.)

(**PUPPET-ALFONSO** lights a cigarette. As he exhales, smoke comes out of his mouth.)

(**PUPPET-SONYA** appears again.)

(Captioned.) Guess what?

PUPPET-ALFONSO. (Captioned.) What?

PUPPET-SONYA. (Turning to her side to reveal a bump, captioned.) I'm pregnant!

PUPPET-ALFONSO. (Captioned.) I'm gonna be a dad!

(**PUPPET-ALFONSO** drops to his knees and kisses **PUPPET-SONYA**'s bump.)

PUPPET-SONYA. (Captioned.) If you're gonna be a dad you're gonna have to quit smoking.

(**SONYA**'s hand appears in the puppet theatre and takes the cigarette from **PUPPET-ALFONSO**.)

(**PUPPET-ALFONSO** gets down on one knee.)

PUPPET-ALFONSO. (Captioned.) Will you marry me?

PUPPET-SONYA. (Captioned.) Yes!

(They dance.)

(They rise up out of view.)

(We then see the real **ALFONSO** and **SONYA** appear, their heads inside the puppet theatre. They appear large on the gauze.)

(As they speak to each other, surtitles appear on the gauze.)

ALFONSO. The show went well, don't you think?

SONYA. Not bad, although you made a few mistakes.

ALFONSO. Do you think anyone noticed?

SONYA. I think you got away with it, as always.

ALFONSO. Is it safe to keep performing?

SONYA. Why wouldn't it be safe?

ALFONSO. Gatherings are prohibited.

SONYA. So?

ALFONSO. Our show is a gathering. Look.

(They look out at the audience.)

All those people sitting there. It's dangerous. They could all be killed and it'd be our fault.

SONYA. At least they'd die laughing.

ALFONSO. Maybe we should pack up for the day.

SONYA. How much money did we make?

ALFONSO. Enough to buy dinner and a bottle of wine.

SONYA. You know I can't drink.

ALFONSO. Ah, the baby won't mind.

SONYA. I need to take a bath.

ALFONSO. I'll join you.

SONYA. Alfonso, stop! There are children here.

ALFONSO. Where?

SONYA. There. In the front row. Petya.

ALFONSO. Petya?

SONYA. My little cousin.

(They look out directly at the camera.)

ALFONSO. Ah yes, Petya! But he can't hear.

SONYA. Yes but he can lip-read.

ALFONSO. Shit. *(To camera.)* Hey! Petya! Time to go home.

SONYA. Ah, look at him. He wants another story. How could you say no to that face?

ALFONSO. What should we do?

SONYA. Tell him what happened next. In the town square.

ALFONSO. Okay. *(To camera.)* Hey, Petya! Watch. Our country is the stage...

> *(**ALFONSO** and **SONYA** leave the puppet theatre.)*
>
> *(A blackout curtain lowers behind the gauze, hiding the stage.)*
>
> *(A puppet-sized puppet theatre is placed in the middle of the puppet theatre.)*
>
> *(A tree is lowered into the puppet theatre.)*
>
> *(A lamppost is lowered into the puppet theatre.)*
>
> *(A bench is lowered into the puppet theatre.)*
>
> *(**PUPPET-ALFONSO** and **PUPPET-SONYA** are positioned behind the puppet-sized puppet theatre.)*
>
> *(A puppet of a townsperson is lowered into the scene, watching the puppet theatre. This is **MOMMA GALYA**.)*
>
> *(A puppet of a townsperson is lowered into the scene, watching the puppet theatre. This is one of Galya's girls: **KATE**.)*

(Another townsperson-puppet is lowered into the scene. This is another of Galya's girls: **LISA***.)*

(Another puppet of a townsperson is lowered into the scene. This is **PAVEL***.)*

(A puppet of a small boy is placed on the bench facing the puppet theatre. This is **PETYA***.)*

(We are in the town square of Vasenka.)

(Then: A jeep is placed in the puppet theatre.)

(A **PUPPET-SOLDIER** *exits the jeep and approaches* **PETYA***.)*

PUPPET-SOLDIER. *(Captioned.)* Disperse immediately! You! Boy! Assemblies are officially prohibited. Do you understand what that means? It means you need to go home. Now!

　　　　(Pause.)

What's wrong with you? I'm telling you to go home.

　　　　(No reaction.)

Are you deaf?

(The **PUPPET-SOLDIER** *raises his gun and points it at the camera.)*

(Sudden flash of light.)

(Blackout.)

(A loud sub sound rumbles through the audience. This should be more felt than heard.)

(In darkness, the gauze rises.)

(Lights up.)

(Silence.)

(Everything of the town square that appeared in the puppet theatre is now visible onstage: the puppet theatre, the **TOWNSPEOPLE**, *a tree, a jeep etc. and the* **SOLDIER** *with his gun raised.)*

(On the ground, a dead child, **PETYA** – *the child is a life-sized puppet.)*

(In silence: a loud scene.)

*(***SONYA** *moves towards* **PETYA***'s body.)*

(All [bracketed] dialogue is inaudible.)

SONYA. [Petya!]

(The surtitle sign reads:)

[inaudible]

(The others watch **SONYA** *lie down next to* **PETYA***.)*

SOLDIER. [He wasn't listening. He wasn't listening! You saw. There are rules.]

KATE. [What did you do?]

SOLDIER. [There are rules.]

KATE. [What are you talking about?]

SOLDIER. [He shouldn't be here. If he wasn't here that wouldn't have happened.]

LISA. [What the fuck did you just do?]

SOLDIER. [He wasn't listening.]

LISA. [Stop saying that!]

SOLDIER. [But there are rules. You have to follow the rules.]

KATE. [He's only a child.]

SOLDIER. [It doesn't matter.]

PAVEL. [He's ten years old!]

SOLDIER. [I gave an order but he wasn't listening.]

ALFONSO. [He's deaf!]

SOLDIER. [What?]

ALFONSO. [He's deaf! He couldn't hear you because he's fucking deaf!]

SOLDIER. *(Turning to point gun at* **ALFONSO***.)* [If you take one more step towards me I will shoot you in the face.]

> *(***LISA*** attacks the* **SOLDIER***. He hits her and she falls to the floor.)*

[Are you out of your fucking mind!]

GALYA. [It's okay! It's okay! She doesn't know what she's doing! She didn't mean it!]

SOLDIER. [What is wrong with you people? Do you want to get shot?]

GALYA. [No! Don't shoot. Put the gun down. Please! I'll take her away! I'll take them all away.]

SOLDIER. [And you! Fuck off before I put a bullet in you.]

KATE. [I'm going!]

SOLDIER. [What are you two doing?]

> *(The* **SOLDIER** *hits* **PAVEL** *and he falls to the floor.)*

(To **ALFONSO***.)* [I've told you to go!]

ALFONSO. [That's my wife! Please!]

SOLDIER. [Who's your wife?]

ALFONSO. [Her!]

SOLDIER. [The weird bitch?]

ALFONSO. [Let me help her! Let me help my wife. Please!]

SOLDIER. [Get her out of here. Now!] *(To* **GALYA** *and others.)* [And you lot. I thought I told you to fuck off. All of you! Go! Now!]

GALYA. [We're gone. We're gone.]

> *(***GALYA** *exits along with* **LISA** *and* **KATE***.)*

SOLDIER. *(To* **PAVEL***.)* [Oi! Sleepy head! Fuck off! Fuck off or die!]

> *(***PAVEL** *runs away.)*

> *(***SOLDIER** *turns to* **ALFONSO** *and* **SONYA***.)*

[This is your last chance.]

> *(The* **SOLDIER** *points the gun at them.)*

> *(They do not move.)*

> *(The* **SOLDIER** *raises his gun upwards and fires two shots in the air. We see the flashes but hear no sound.)*

> *(***ALFONSO** *drags* **SONYA** *away from* **PETYA***.)*

> *(They exit, leaving the* **SOLDIER** *standing over* **PETYA***'s body.)*

> *(Snow falls.)*

> *(***SOLDIER** *looks at* **PETYA** *then he looks at the audience.)*

(Captioned.) Oh. You're still here? You shouldn't be. None of you should be here. You shouldn't be here. And you shouldn't be here. And you shouldn't be here and that boy shouldn't have been here. You know the orders. Why did you even come? To see a show? Well the show's over. Do you understand? There's nothing to see. So you might as well go home. Go home or get arrested.

> *(Wires lower from above.)*

> *(The **SOLDIER** lifts **PETYA** and attaches him to the wires. He watches as **PETYA** rises up and out of view.)*

> *(He lights a cigarette and turns back to the audience.)*

You're not getting the message are you? I said go home. You do know why we banned these gatherings? For your own safety. To protect you from the person sitting next to you. You don't know who they are. Not really. You assume they're like you. You assume they have the same values, the same politics. But really you have no idea. For all you know, they're your enemy. And that's why I'm here. To protect you. And anyone who refuses my protection will be shot. Maybe I'm not being clear enough. I'm trying my best. I'll even show you the gun I'll shoot you with. This one. This is the gun I will shoot you with if you disobey my orders. Is *that* clear enough? I'm making this as accessible as I can. Look, there's even surtitles. You see, I want everyone to understand everything! I'm like that. So this is your last chance. Go home or get shot with this gun.

> *(Silence.)*

What the fuck is wrong with you people? You can't just sit there in silence. Say something.

*(**ALFONSO** has moved forward to the middle of the stage.)*

You. Speak.

(Nothing.)

*(**SOLDIER** turns to **ALFONSO** and holds a gun to his head.)*

Speak!

*(**ALFONSO** signs and **SONYA** speaks.)*

ALFONSO. *(Signed.)* Our country woke up the next morning and refused to hear the soldiers.

SOLDIER. *(Captioned.)* I told you to speak!

ALFONSO. *(Signed.)* In the name of Petya, we refuse.

SOLDIER. *(Captioned.)* Why won't you speak?

ALFONSO. *(Signed.)* My people, you were really something fucking fine that first morning.

SOLDIER. *(Captioned.)* Why are you ignoring me? What's wrong with you all?

ALFONSO. *(Signed.)* Once frightened, bound to your beds, you now stand up like human masts.

SOLDIER. *(Captioned.)* Wait – why is that sign moving?

*(The **TOWNSPEOPLE** have entered and move to the caption screen which starts lowering to stage level.)*

ALFONSO. *(Signed.)* Deafness passes through us like a police whistle.

SOLDIER. *(Captioned.)* What are you doing? That's my sign. You can't take my sign. That's where my words go.

(The **TOWNSPEOPLE** *unplug the sign and carry it to another place on stage.)*

ALFONSO. *(Signed.)* At six a.m. when soldiers compliment girls in the alleyway, the girls slide by, pointing to their ears. At eight, the bakery door is shut in soldier Ivanoff's face, though he's their best customer. At ten Momma Galya makes a sign for the soldiers to see – a flag for our newly formed deaf republic.

(By now, the caption screen has becomes a traffic road sign.)

*(***GALYA** *changes the sign to read:)*

THE PEOPLE ARE DEAF

Our hearing doesn't weaken, but something silent in us strengthens.

*(***EVERYONE** *moves to stand around the sign.)*

Deafness, an insurgency, begins.

(The **SOLDIER** *tries to speak.)*

SOLDIER. You're all under –

(The **CITIZENS** *all point to their ears.)*

(Pause.)

*(***SOLDIER** *goes over to the caption screen and changes the text.)*

(They caption screen reads:)

Okay, Fine.

If you really can't hear me.

Then there must be something wrong with you.

So.

New rules.

All citizens are required to volunteer themselves for an
official ear inspection.

Anyone who refuses to have their ears voluntarily
examined will be arrested.

The hearing test is about to begin.

Are you ready?

3

2

1

(Pause.)

(Captioned.) Helllooooo?

(No reaction.)

HELLLLOOOOOOO!!!??

(No reaction.)

CAN ANYONE HEAR ME?????

(No reaction.)

(Pause.)

There's an old joke... A man walks into a grocer's
and says, "How old do you think I am?" Grocer takes
a look at the man and says, "I dunno – sixty?" Man
says, "No, I'm eighty. Got loads of work done, hair,
teeth, facelift..." Next the man's at the butcher's and
he goes to the butcher, "How old do you think I am?"
Butcher says, "No idea. Maybe sixty?" Man says, "I'm
eighty would you believe it – got my hair done, teeth,
facelift..." Later, the man's at the bus stop and he sees
this little old lady so he asks her, "How old do you think
I am?" and the old lady says, "Let me feel your balls".

The man's a bit confused but says okay and lowers his trousers. The old lady rolls up her sleeves, has a good rummage of his nuts then says "You're eighty." Man says, "How the fuck did you know that??" and the old lady says, "I was standing behind you in the butchers."

(*No reaction.*)

Jesus Christ, not a single laugh! That's fucking great material! What is *wrong* with you people?

(**SOLDIER** *goes to his jeep and turns on the radio.*)

(*Really loud music. Rock 'n' Roll.**)

(*The caption sign reads:*)

Rock Music Plays

(*The* **CITIZENS** *look at the sign and shrug their shoulders.*)

(**SOLDIER** *looks at them expecting a reaction.*)

(*No reaction.*)

(*The* **SOLDIER** *goes back to the jeep.*)

(*He changes the radio station. Hip-hop.*)

(*The caption sign reads:*)

Hip Hop Plays

(*The* **SOLDIER** *looks at them. He tries to dance, encouraging them to join.*)

---

* A licence to produce *Deaf Republic* does not include a performance licence for any third-party or copyrighted music. Licensees should create an original composition or use music in the public domain. For further information, please see the Music Use Note on page iii.

(The **CITIZENS** *disperse around the town square, smoking, sitting, drinking coffee, ignoring the* **SOLDIER**.*)*

*(***SOLDIER** *changes the radio again. Death Metal.)*

(The caption sign reads:)

Death Metal Plays

(The **SOLDIER** *emerges from the jeep with an endoscopy camera and moves towards* **SONYA**. *He forces* **SONYA** *to the floor.)*

(He holds the camera to her ear.)

(The gauze lowers.)

(On it, we see the live image of a giant ear.)

(The camera moves in closer.)

(And closer.)

(The camera moves inside her ear: the screen goes white.)

(The music changes.)

(On the gauze we see:)

Of Weddings before the War

(We zoom out of her ear and we see **SONYA** *in a wedding dress.)*

(The town square is garlanded with lights, strung around the tree and between the tree and the lamppost.)

(A summer's evening.)

(The soldier's jeep is not there, and there is a crate of beers sitting by the bench.)

(As the camera zooms out of **SONYA**'*s ear we find her and* **ALFONSO** *looking at each other, faces close, smiling.* **ALFONSO** *then moves away, gets a microphone, and prepares for a speech.)*

*(***SONYA** *signs to the camera.)*

SONYA. *(Signed, captioned.)* Hey, Petya! Look! I think he's about to give a speech...

*(***ALFONSO** *speaks,* **SONYA** *signs.)*

ALFONSO. *(To audience.)* Hello. Thanks for coming.

It's amazing to see so many of you here.

We didn't know who to invite so we just invited everyone!

The whole town!!

But we didn't think you'd all actually come!!!

Hopefully we've got enough wine.

Erm...

I've written a poem – what?

SONYA. Slow down. I'm signing for Petya.

ALFONSO. Of course! Petya! How could I forget?

*(***ALFONSO** *moves over to Petya and signs to the camera.)*

(Signed.) Hey buddy! Good to see you!

*(***ALFONSO** *moves away to continue his speech.)*

(Spoken.) Erm... What was I saying? Yes. I've written a poem. So anyway...yes...

>   *(Pause.)*

Yes, I bought you a wedding dress big enough for the two of us
and in the taxi home
we kissed a coin from your mouth to mine.

You are two fingers more beautiful than any other woman –
I am not a poet, Sonya.
I want to live in your hair.

You leapt on my back, I
ran to the bath,
and yes, I slipped on the wet floor –

I watched you gleam in the shower
holding your
breasts in your hand –

two small explosions.

>   *(Applause and cheers.* **SONYA** *moves to* **ALFONSO**.*)*

>   *(***KATE** *and* **LISA** *approach the camera, appearing large on the gauze. Petya reads their lips. Their dialogue is captioned.)*

KATE. *(Spoken, captioned.)* Oh, he's so cute!

LISA. Look at his face.

KATE. Hey, Petya? Want to dance?

LISA. Don't dance with her – dance with me!

KATE. It's up to you, Petya. You can choose. Who do you think is prettier?

LISA. Stop, you're making him shy.

KATE. Okay, fine. Who's the best puppeteer? That's the real question.

LISA. *(With gestures.)* Yeah, Petya, who's your favourite me or her?

KATE. Wait – can you sign?

LISA. Not really, but what can I say – I'm gifted with my hands.

KATE. Whatever. I'm sure he's much happier reading my lips.

GALYA. That's enough, girls. Leave the poor boy alone.

> *(**GALYA** is there. **KATE** and **LISA** move away.)*

> *(The **GUESTS** dance.)*

(Captioned.) Don't mind them. They're probably drunk. I hope not because they're supposed to do a show later and everyone will see. You can't hide behind a puppet, Petya. If your hands wobble, the strings wobble, and the game's up, and you can't tell your story. I'm not one to talk. These hands. Not what they used to be.

> *(The camera of Petya's gaze moves to **GALYA**'s hands.)*

It's not the drink has done it. But time. You see this? It's called the life line. Mine ended years ago. But enough of that. Oh, Petya. What a handsome young man you are! You even brushed your hair for the occasion! Impressive. How old are you now? So grown up. Isn't this a happy day? It wasn't long ago that we couldn't do this. But now. Peace. You know what peace is? Silence...

> *(The camera focuses on **GALYA**'s mouth, lip reading her words.)*

What are you looking at? My mouth? Am I speaking clearly enough for you? What do you see here? In my open mouth. Ah. The nakedness of a whole nation. These words. They weigh, Petya. The stories I could tell. The things I've seen...

(Camera moves up to **GALYA***'s eyes.)*

This body I testify from is a binoculars through which you watch, God. He watches through us, Petya. Through you too. You can't hear, but you observe. You witness. Keep watching. You never know what you might see...

(The camera focuses on her breasts, mesmerised.)

Oi! Cheeky pup. That's not what I meant. But you've got the right idea. Stay alert! Pay attention! We see what you see. Oh, look! The happy couple!

*(***GALYA*** points and the camera follows in the direction and finds* **SONYA** *and* **ALFONSO** *kissing.)*

ALFONSO. *(Captioned – mouth full of his wife's lips.)* I love you.

SONYA. *(Captioned.)* Stop talking while we're kissing.

(The camera moves from their mouths and focuses on **SONYA***'s ear.)*

(Blackout curtain lowers behind the gauze.)

(The camera moves in closer to **SONYA***'s ear.)*

(And closer.)

(The camera moves inside her ear: the screen goes white.)

(We zoom out of her ear and we are back at the military checkpoint, with the **SOLDIER** *inspecting the* **CITIZENS**' *ears.)*

(Blackout curtain rises.)

(The **SOLDIER** *is standing over* **SONYA**, *holding the endoscopy camera. He puts the camera back in the jeep, then changes the text on the road sign:)*

DEAFNESS IS A CONTAGIOUS DISEASE.

FOR YOUR OWN PROTECTION ALL SUBJECTS IN CONTAMINATED AREAS MUST SURRENDER TO BE QUARANTINED WITHIN 24 HOURS.

(The **SOLDIER** *exits.)*

(The **CITIZENS** *are alone.)*

(Everyone watches **SONYA** *as she slowly sits up, composes herself and begins to sign.)*

(This scene is signed only and takes place mostly in silence.)

SONYA. *(Signed.)* Soldier.

KATE. Soldier.

LISA. Soldier.

ALFONSO. Soldier.

GALYA. *(Signed and spoken.)* Soldier.

SONYA. Yes. Good. This is the sign for "soldier".

GALYA. *(Signed and spoken.)* Soldier.

SONYA. And this is the sign for "hide".

KATE. Hide.

LISA. Hide.

ALFONSO. Hide.

PAVEL. Hide.

GALYA. *(Signed and spoken.)* Hide.

SONYA. Nearly. Hands together. Like this. Hide.

> *(**SONYA** goes to **GALYA** to help, taking hold of her hands. **GALYA**'s hands shake.)*
>
> *(**GALYA** gives up and takes out a knife. She sits down and starts carving a puppet.)*

Is she okay?

LISA. Don't mind her.

SONYA. Okay. So. Plane. This is the sign for "plane". And this is the sign for "bomb".

LISA. Bomb.

KATE. Bomb.

LISA. Wait – I thought this was the sign for bomb.

KATE. What, this?

LISA. Yeah.

KATE. Okay. Bomb.

ALFONSO. No, no, that's the verb.

LISA. What?

ALFONSO. You're thinking of the verb – bombing – That's the noun: bomb.

LISA. Okay.

KATE. But maybe we should use something a bit more dramatic like BOMB!

ALFONSO. Depends what you wanna say and the context and all that but to be honest I kinda prefer using a sort of hand-grenade more like *(Throws grenade.)*...

>   (**ALFONSO** *lets out a plume of cigarette smoke as the grenade lands.)*

KATE. Yes! Love it!

LISA. Yeah, or maybe even with a bazooka so you can really fucking go BOMB!!!!

SONYA. Hey! Hey! Hey! I'm the fucking teacher here and I can't teach them twenty signs for the word bomb, that's not gonna work, I have to pick *one* sign and start there or else their heads will be overloaded and they won't learn a thing, like look at this guy here in the front row he's doing his best but he's not got a clue what we're signing about so I need to pick one fucking sign and try to teach that or we'll never get anywhere, okay?

LISA, ALFONSO, KATE & GALYA. Fair enough, yeah, okay.

>   *(Pause.)*

SONYA. So –

PAVEL. *(Raising his hand, speaks, captioned.)* I have a question.

>   *(Everyone looks at* **PAVEL**. *Then everyone turns to look at the caption screen.)*

(Spoken, captioned.) I think I need some help.

>   *(Everyone looks at* **PAVEL**.*)*

SONYA. *(Signed.)* With what?

PAVEL. *(Spoken, captioned.)* Well, the signing, but also in general, the whole...pretending to be deaf.

>   *(Everyone looks at the caption screen. Then everyone looks at* **PAVEL**.*)*

LISA. *(Signed.)* Pretending?

PAVEL. *(Spoken, captioned.)* That's what we're doing, isn't it? Since Petya died?

> *(Everyone looks at the caption screen. Then everyone looks at* **PAVEL**.*)*

LISA. *(Signed.)* I'm not pretending.

ALFONSO. *(Signed.)* Me neither.

PAVEL. *(Spoken, captioned.)* Wait – you're actually deaf?

> *(Everyone looks at the caption screen. Then everyone looks at* **PAVEL**.*)*

ALFONSO. *(Signed.)* Of course.

LISA. *(Signed.)* And not just us. The whole town. *(To audience.)* Everyone here. No one can hear you.

SONYA. *(Signed.)* Why would we be pretending to be deaf?

ALFONSO. *(Signed.)* That sounds pretty offensive, man.

PAVEL. *(Spoken, captioned.)* No, no. Totally, yeah. No way. Totally. Bad vibe. Yeah. Sorry.

> *(The rest of them move away, kind of annoyed at him.* **SONYA** *continues teaching sign to the others.)*
>
> *(***PAVEL** *moves to stand next to the screen,* **LISA** *is on the other side of the stage. He looks across to her.)*

(Spoken, captioned.) I didn't mean to be offensive.

> *(***LISA** *reads the sign. They stand on either side of the sign.)*

LISA. *(Signed.)* Don't worry. You'll get it.

PAVEL. *(Spoken, captioned.)* Thanks.

(Pause.)

PAVEL. *(Spoken, captioned.)* So, just to be sure...you literally just went deaf?

LISA. *(Signed.)* Yeah.

PAVEL. *(Spoken, captioned.)* Wild.

LISA. *(Signed.)* And I know it sounds strange but it feels like I've been deaf my whole life.

PAVEL. *(Spoken, captioned.)* So could you...give me some tips?

LISA. *(Signed.)* Well, for one, you need to remember to look into peoples' eyes.

> **(PAVEL** *is following on the caption screen, then abruptly changes to look at* **LISA**.*)*

PAVEL. *(Spoken, captioned.)* Oh, right. Absolutely. Yes.

> *(Pause.)*

(Spoken, captioned.) Why?

LISA. *(Signed.)* Well if you're lip reading or someone's signing – you can't *pretend* to be listening – you've got to actually look at them! You have to pay attention. I guess what I'm saying is, people will know you're deaf, because you'll be the only one listening.

PAVEL. *(Spoken, captioned.)* So you mean, now we're deaf, everything matters?

LISA. *(Signed.)* Something like that.

PAVEL. *(Spoken, captioned.)* Sounds exhausting.

LISA. *(Signed.)* And you really are gonna have to learn sign language.

PAVEL. *(Spoken, captioned.)* I know. I'm trying. Look: *(Signs and speaks.)* The Soldier shot Petya.

LISA. *(Signed.)* Nearly. But you've got to show the *positions* of the signs. There isn't just shooting and dying, someone has to do the shooting and someone has to do the dying, you know what I mean?

PAVEL. *(Spoken, captioned.)* Someone has to do the kissing, that sort of thing?

LISA. *(Signed.)* What?

PAVEL. *(Spoken, captioned.)* Nothing. Bad joke.

LISA. *(Signed.)* The point is, you can't just be a passive observer. You have to take a position. So, for example, I couldn't just sort of be standing outside a story like this, facing out and narrating to an audience in some abstract kind of way. In sign, there is no "narrator" in the traditional sense, and there's definitely no "audience". You don't just tell a story, you're *in* the story. We're all in the story.

> *(The gauze lowers with the blackout curtain behind it.)*
>
> *(**SONYA**'s hands appear in the puppet theatre.)*
>
> *(Her hands appear large on the screen. She continues to teach the townspeople sign language – her hands overlaying the stage.)*
>
> *(She makes the sign for "Hide".)*
>
> *(She makes the sign for "Plane".)*
>
> *(She makes the sign for "Bomb".)*
>
> *(Suddenly a deep bass sound moves through the theatre.)*
>
> *(We see **SONYA**'s hands remove all small objects from the puppet theatre.)*

(The puppet theatre is empty.)

(In the puppet theatre, we see a room being constructed: a bath, a window, a chair, a cot.)

(PUPPET-SONYA *is placed in the bath.)*

(PUPPET-ALFONSO *is placed in the chair, a baby in his arms.)*

(On the gauze we see:)

What is a child?

A quiet between two bombardments

(The blackout curtain rises and we find **SONYA** *and* **ALFONSO** *in their apartment.)*

*(**SONYA** is in the bath.)*

*(**ALFONSO** is sitting in the chair, holding their newborn, **ANUSHKA**.)*

(They sign. The surtitles appear on the gauze.)

SONYA. Get in with me.

ALFONSO. You know what happened last time you said that?

SONYA. What?

ALFONSO. *(Gestures to the baby.)* This!

SONYA. I'm not trying to seduce you.

ALFONSO. What then?

SONYA. A man should smell better than his country.

ALFONSO. Ah.

(A low sound. A rumbling.)

SONYA. Did you notice that? The shelling.

ALFONSO. Yeah. You can hear it?

SONYA. Of course not. But I hate that I can feel it.

ALFONSO. I'll tape the windows. Protect the glass.

> (**ALFONSO** *places* **ANUSHKA** *into the cot.*)

> (*He tapes the window.*)

> (*The camera films the window as the tape is applied.*)

You okay?

SONYA. Where are we?

ALFONSO. What do you mean?

SONYA. We have no past. It is obliterated.

We have no future. It is unthinkable.

We just have this. Condemned to the present tense.

ALFONSO. It's my honour to be present with you.

> (*Pause.*)

SONYA. I am of deaf people and I have no country but a bathtub and an infant and a marriage bed!

> (*Pause.*)

ALFONSO. There. That should keep the glass from shattering.

> (*On the gauze the tape appears large, taping the whole stage.*)

SONYA. In you get.

> (**ALFONSO** *undresses and gets into the bath with* **SONYA**.)

Pig. Here.

(**SONYA** *throws a sponge over to* **ALFONSO**.)

ALFONSO. Thank you.

(*He looks at her. They kiss.*)

You can fuck anyone – but with whom can you sit in water?

SONYA. That's lovely but – I'm getting out.

ALFONSO. Why?

SONYA. Anushka's crying.

ALFONSO. You can hear her?

SONYA. Of course not. But I love that I can feel it.

(**SONYA** *gets out of the bath. She dresses herself and sits with* **ANUSHKA**.)

(*At another part of the stage – on a bench – two citizens meet up. They are* **GALYA'S GIRLS**.)

(*We don't see them directly but they appear livestreamed onto the gauze.*)

(*They sign.*)

KATE. (*Signed, captioned.*) No one can see us.

LISA. What?

KATE. Invisible. We...invisible.

LISA. Okay you need to pay more attention when Sonya's teaching. You're signing's fucked!

KATE. I'm saying: no one can see us. Out there. The world. Forgotten. We – we – how do I sign "a-r-e"?

LISA. You don't! Small words like "is" – "and" – "are" – those words become movements, facial expressions, directions.

KATE. Okay.

LISA. Sign language has its own structure, its own grammar – a lot of the time the order of words is different. For example, instead of signing What's-Your-Name, you'd sign:

(**LISA** *signs,* **SONYA** *speaks.*)

SONYA. *(To* **ANUSHKA**.*)* Your-Name-What.

LISA. *(Signed.)* Which if someone spoke out loud in English would sound pretty funny! No one speaks like that.

KATE. Poets, maybe.

LISA. That's right! In a sense, sign language *is* poetry. We're poets now!

KATE. What good is that?

LISA. It's a new way of thinking!

Watch –
Vasenka citizens do not know they are evidence of happiness.

In time of war,
each is a ripped-out document of laughter.

Watch God –
deaf have something to tell
that not even they can hear.

Climb a roof in Central Square of this bombarded city,
you will see –
one neighbour thieves a cigarette,
another gives a dog
a pint of sunlit beer.

You will find me, God,
like a dumb pigeon's beak, I am
pecking
every which way at astonishment.

KATE. Beautiful.

>   (**GALYA** *is there.*)

GALYA. (*Signed.*) Go home girls. They're arresting people.
Your poems are no match for a man with a machine
gun.

>   (*We are back with* **ALFONSO** *and* **SONYA**.)

>   (**SONYA** *is nursing* **ANUSHKA**.)

>   (*The camera is focused on* **SONYA**'*s face.*)

ALFONSO. (*Signing, captioned.*) You step out of the bath
and the entire nation calms –

a drop of lemon-egg shampoo,
you smell like bees,

a brief kiss,
I don't know anything about you – except the spray of
freckles on your shoulders!

which makes me feel so thrillingly

alone.

>   (**ALFONSO** *stands up, naked, facing* **SONYA**.)

I stand on earth

penis sticking out –
for years

in your direction.

SONYA. (*Spoken, to* **ANUSHKA**.) Doesn't Daddy talks
funny yes he does yes he does funny Daddy with his
funny words funny silly goose Daddy.

ALFONSO. (*Signed, captioned.*) Maybe you're the poet.

>   (**ALFONSO** *steps out of the bath.*)

(The camera moves down into the bath. We see the water on the gauze.)

*(**ALFONSO** dresses.)*

SONYA. Ouch.

ALFONSO. You okay?

SONYA. She must be starving.

ALFONSO. I know the feeling.

SONYA. You too?

ALFONSO. It won't be the bombs that kill us.

SONYA. Come.

ALFONSO. What?

SONYA. She won't mind.

ALFONSO. I can't.

SONYA. You can share.

ALFONSO. I'm not taking my child's milk!

SONYA. Come. Taste.

> *(**SONYA** holds out a finger with a pearl of milk. **ALFONSO** puts it to his lips.)*

ALFONSO. It's warm.

SONYA. Maybe you should try to sleep. When you're asleep, you don't need to eat.

ALFONSO. No.

> *(**ALFONSO** moves to the door and puts on his coat.)*

I'm going to find bread. I won't be long.

> *(The gauze rises.)*

*(**ALFONSO** signs. **SONYA** speaks.)*

ALFONSO. *(To audience.)* I was going to tell you what happened next but you already know.

You were there.

You saw what happened.

> *(The apartment separates to reveal the* **SOLDIER** *standing there.)*

You watch from your windows as four jeeps pull onto the curb: peeking from behind curtains you saw how Sonya was stolen into a jeep as Anushka cried, left behind as the convoy rattled away.

You saw how they shoved Sonya into the army jeep, one morning, one morning in May, one dime-bright morning –

they shove her
and she zigzags and turns and trips in silence

which is a soul's noise.

> *(As* **ALFONSO** *signs and* **SONYA** *speaks, we see* **SONYA** *dragged to the town square.)*

You saw her taken to the town square, blindfolded, put in front of a firing squad.

But I didn't see any of it.

Because I wasn't there.

I wasn't there for Sonya. I'd gone to find bread.

So whatever happened, it's my fault.

It's my fault for not being there.

Because if I'd been there none of this would have happened. This scene wouldn't be in the story. It would all be different but because I wasn't there the soldiers raised their guns. And then Sonya spoke. She said

(Unsigned, captioned.) Ready!

She spoke in a voice I cannot hear and said ready and I only know this because you told me because you were there.

you were all there watching

you saw what happened

you were there and I wasn't

I wasn't there with my wife

Forgive me

I love you, Sonya

I love you too, Alfonso

> *(Pause.)*

Wait – can you hear me?

> *(**ALFONSO** looks to the stage.)*

> *(**SONYA** looks at **ALFONSO**.)*

SONYA. *(Unsigned, captioned.)* No.

> *(Gunshot.)*

> *(**SONYA** is shot. She collapses.)*

I can't hear you, darling. I'm dead.

> *(The **SOLDIER** exits.)*

> *(It is snowing.)*

> *(**ALFONSO** moves to **SONYA**'s body.)*

> *(**GALYA** enters, followed by **KATE**, **LISA** and **PAVEL**.)*

> *(They stand around **ALFONSO**.)*

(**ALFONSO** *signs.* **SONYA** *speaks.*)

ALFONSO. *(Signed.)* We are gathered here today to celebrate
the life of Sonya Barabinski.

I've prepared some words.

They might come out strange, because everything feels
strange.

But –

> (**ALFONSO** *moves forward.*)

> *(Wires lower and the others attach them to*
> **SONYA**. *During Alfonso's poem she's raised*
> *out of view.)*

> *(Again,* **ALFONSO** *signs.* **SONYA** *speaks.)*

I, this body into which the hand of God plunges,
empty-chested stand.

You left, my door-slamming wife; and I,
A fool live.

But the voice I don't hear when I speak to myself is the
clearest voice:
when my wife washed my hair, when I kissed

between her toes –
in the empty streets of our districts, a bit of wind

called for life.

It's the air. Something in the air wants us too much.

> (**SONYA** *is gone.*)

> (**ALFONSO** *moves over to the puppet theatre*
> *and holds* **PUPPET-SONYA** *in his arms.*)

> (**GALYA** *watches.*)

*(**KATE** signs to **LISA** – "I'll see you later" – and exits.)*

*(**PAVEL** and **LISA** remain – **PAVEL** is at the back of the stage setting up the camera. He turns to look at **LISA**.)*

(They sign.)

LISA. What's the camera for?

PAVEL. For evidence.

LISA. Oh.

PAVEL. Are you OK?

LISA. Not really.

PAVEL. Same.

LISA. Your signing's getting better, though!

PAVEL. I'm trying.

LISA. You know, I don't know your name.

PAVEL. It's Pavel.

LISA. No, I mean your sign name. Mine's this *(She signs her name.)* – because I'm a warrior.

PAVEL. Cool. What should mine be?

LISA. Hmm. You smoke, right? So we can take the Ukrainian P for Pavel, and do something like this...

PAVEL. So we can use signs from other languages?

LISA. For our names, yeah. Mixing different alphabets – BSL, Ukrainian sign, whatever – so the soldiers can't understand us.

PAVEL. *That's* why Galya's signs are so confusing.

LISA. No, they're just confusing.

PAVEL. Right.

> *(Pause.)*

LISA. What kind of evidence?

PAVEL. What?

LISA. You said the camera was for evidence. Evidence of what?

PAVEL. Our suffering.

LISA. What about our tenderness?

PAVEL. Our what?

LISA. Our tenderness.

PAVEL. I don't know that sign.

> *(**LISA** touches **PAVEL**'s face.)*

LISA. I'll see you around, Pavel.

> *(**LISA** exits in the direction of **KATE**.)*
>
> *(**PAVEL** exits in the other direction.)*
>
> *(**ALFONSO** appears behind the puppet theatre.)*
>
> *(The screen lowers.)*
>
> *(On the screen, we see **PUPPET-SONYA** lying lifeless on the floor.)*
>
> *(**PUPPET-ALFONSO** kneels over her. He weeps.)*
>
> *(**PUPPET-GALYA** arrives.)*
>
> *(Surtitles appear on the gauze. No spoken dialogue, just text.)*

PUPPET-GALYA. Time to go home, Alfonso. It's past curfew.

PUPPET-ALFONSO. I have to do the show.

PUPPET-GALYA. Everyone's gone. Go home. It's dangerous.

PUPPET-ALFONSO. I hope she can hear me. I hope she can see me.

PUPPET-GALYA. I'm sure she can. And Petya. And all our dead. They're still with us. They're still here. Watching.

PUPPET-ALFONSO. We're going to lose. We were always going to lose.

PUPPET-GALYA. No. We can fight.

PUPPET-ALFONSO. How? With our hands? With our ears?

PUPPET-GALYA. There are ways.

PUPPET-ALFONSO. I suppose I can always gather the soldiers together for a poetry reading. Bore them to death.

PUPPET-GALYA. I have a plan. Trust me. But first – you must go home. Your baby needs you. I'll pack up the theatre. Go.

> (**ALFONSO** *leaves the stage. He takes* **PUPPET-SONYA** *with him.*)

> (**PUPPET-GALYA** *watches them go and then exits.*)

> (*The blackout curtain lowers.*)

> (*In the puppet theatre, we see the apartment being constructed once again: the bath, window, chair, and cot.*)

> (*On the gauze the image cross fades to a child's mobile toy hanging in the air. A selection of animals.*)

> (**ALFONSO***'s face appears on the screen. The camera is in the cot – we see* **ALFONSO** *from the baby's POV.*)

(He stands over the cot, and signs to his infant.)

ALFONSO. *(Signs.)* Little daughter
rainwater

snow and branches protect you
whitewashed walls

and neighbours' hands all
Child of my Aprils

little earth of
Six pounds

my white hair
Keeps your sleep lit

> *(The blackout curtain raises.)*

> *(We are back at Alfonso's apartment.)*

When you grow up, I hope you will be deaf.

So you only pay attention to what really matters.

So you can tune into the music of the world.

So you remember where you came from.

But for now.

We must pretend.

We must pretend, Anushka.

You pretend to be happy and I'll pretend to be the world's greatest poet and Sonya will pretend to be alive.

> *(**ALFONSO** moves away from the cot.)*

> *(He is drinking vodka.)*

> *(He sees **SONYA**'s clothes on the floor.)*

Wife taken, child

not three days out of the womb, in my arms, our apartment
empty, on the floor

the dirty snow from her boots.

(He puts on her dress. He drinks.)

*(**SONYA** emerges from under the bath water.)*

SONYA. Why are you wearing my clothes, silly?

ALFONSO. So I can be close to you.

SONYA. But I'm right here.

ALFONSO. I want you closer. I want you to be alive.

SONYA. You don't need me. You know what to do.

ALFONSO. I am your boy
drowning in this country, who doesn't know the word for drowning

I am diving for the last time!

SONYA. You know what, Alfonso? You might have to pretend that I'm alive, but at least you don't have to pretend to be a poet.

(She disappears underwater.)

(The gauze rises.)

*(**ALFONSO** picks up **ANUSHKA** and steps forward off the apartment.)*

(The apartment slides offstage to reveal:)

*(A **SOLDIER** in the town square. He is surrounded.)*

*(**GALYA** is there, **KATE** and **LISA**, **PAVEL**.)*

(**GALYA** *signs.*)

GALYA. *(Signed, to audience.)* Who wants a public killing?
A public killing in a sunlit piazza!

(*The* **SOLDIER** *begs for mercy.*)

SOLDIER. Please. Please. Have mercy.

(*Everyone points at their ears.*)

GALYA. *(Signed.)* What's that?

SOLDIER. Have mercy on me.

KATE. *(Signed.)* Don't waste your words.

PAVEL. *(Signed.)* The people are deaf!

(**GALYA** *speaks,* **LISA** *signs.*)

LISA. *(Signed.)*
Deafness is suspended above blue tin roofs
And copper eaves; deafness
Feeds on birches, light posts, hospital roofs, bells;
Deafness rests in our men's chests

(**KATE** *spits on the* **SOLDIER.** **LISA** *kicks him.*)

(**GALYA** *holds out a knife, offering it to
anyone willing to finish the job.*)

(**GALYA** *speaks,* **LISA** *signs.*)

GALYA. *(Speaking to audience.)* Who is willing to defend
his country? I'm sure most of you have no idea how to
kill a man. But you have to start somewhere!

(**PAVEL** *takes it.*)

(*He hesitates.*)

(**ALFONSO** *is there.*)

ALFONSO. *(Signed, captioned.)* I'll do it. I'll do it for a box of oranges.

(**ALFONSO** *takes the knife.*)

(*He approaches the* **SOLDIER.**)

SOLDIER. I know you can hear me.

(**ALFONSO** *points at his ear.*)

It's all an act. All of it. Vasenka. What even is that? It's not a real place. You made it up. You made it all up. None of this is real. It's a fiction. You're all actors. And that boy. The deaf child. He didn't die. It was fake. Nothing happened. The dead boy is alive. This war is not a war. And you are not deaf.

(**ALFONSO** *cuts the* **SOLDIER**'s *ear off.*)

(*He throws it to the ground and the* **SOLDIER** *goes to get it.*)

(**ALFONSO** *follows him. He cuts him to the lung, stabbing the* **SOLDIER**. *Over and over.*)

(*The* **OTHERS** *cheer.*)

(*Wires lower. They attach them to the* **SOLDIER**'s *body.*)

(*His corpse is flung around the stage like a lifeless puppet.*)

(*The* **CITIZENS** *celebrate wildly,* **ALFONSO** *frenzied and covered in blood.*)

(*The gauze lowers.*)

(Projected on the gauze:)

At the trial of God, we will ask: why did you allow this?

And the answer will be an echo: why did you allow this?

(Darkness.)

(A sound. A buzzing.)

(A drone takes off and hovers on stage.)

(It flies over the audience and films them.)

(The drone then turns back to the stage, searching.)

*(It finds **ALFONSO**, covered in blood, holding the knife.)*

*(**ALFONSO** stares at the drone, the drone stares at **ALFONSO**.)*

*(Unseen, a **SOLDIER** enters behind **ALFONSO**, raises his gun.)*

*(**ALFONSO** is shot.)*

*(The drone lands in the **SOLDIER**'s hand and they exit.)*

(Snow falls.)

*(**GALYA** enters.)*

(Wires lower.)

*(She attaches them to **ALFONSO** and watches him as he rises out of view.)*

(She notices something in the puppet theatre – it is the baby **ANUSHKA**.*)*

*(***GALYA*** approaches her and picks her up, then moves to the puppet theatre and changes the setting. She removes the tree, the bench, the car, the lamppost, etc.)*

(As she removes these items they fly out on stage, rising up out of view.)

(She then lowers red curtains into the puppet theatre.)

(As she adds the curtains to the puppet theatre they fly in on stage.)

(We are now in Momma Galya's theatre.)

(She notices the audience.)

GALYA. *(Signs.)* Welcome!

(She lowers **PUPPET-LISA** *into the puppet theatre.)*

(At the same time, **LISA** *is lowered onto the stage.)*

(Gauze flies out.)

*(***GALYA*** speaks,* **LISA** *signs.)*

(To audience.) You're all still here? Good! You're very welcome! You're very welcome and you're very welcome and you know you're *very* welcome. You're all very welcome to my little theatre. Before we start let me explain that tonight's show is an accessible performance which means I'll be speaking out loud for those of you who are hearing. I apologise in advance to

the deaf audience members, and hope I don't become
a distraction. I hope my words don't get in the way
of the action. In fact, if possible, I recommend you
try to ignore me. But I know that won't be easy. And
those of you who are hearing...you know who you are.
Soldiers. Yes, yes, there are soldiers here tonight, sitting
amongst us! But please, fellow citizens, don't cause
any trouble. This is a place where we try to put our
differences aside. So, to all you soldiers sitting silently
in this room – I know I haven't always been your best
friend. I may have screamed at you in the street from
time to time, or whipped you with the leash of your
own patrol dog – sorry about that, Lieutenant – but
please believe me when I say everyone's welcome: my
theatre is an accessible space. But a word of warning
to our regular patrons – things have changed since
the...occupation started. We've had to – how shall I
put it? – *broaden* our repertoire. My puppeteers have
had to learn new skills. Trust me, the things they are
capable of will amaze you! But don't worry, they're still
incredibly talented with their hands. Which is more
than you can say for me. Don't talk to me about these
old things. They're useless! My puppets won't even let
me hold them anymore! I'm too shaky! *(Signs this,
badly.)* That's why my signing's so bad. *(Stops signing.)*
But luckily, I have my girls with me. It's a funny job
when you think about it. Interpreting. Just repeating
whatever words I put into her hands. Kind of like a
puppet. Let's see. What should I make her do? Ah, I'm
only joking. Let's get started!

(**GALYA** *moves away to the puppet theatre.*)

(**LISA** *continues to sign, after* **GALYA** *stops
speaking.*)

LISA. *(Signed, uncaptioned.)* She tried to learn sign,
but trust me, you don't want to see it. The other day,
we were doing a puppet show for kids and she was

supposed to sign "I'm the teacher" but actually kept signing "I'm dead". Standing there smiling telling a whole room of traumatised kids that she was dead.

GALYA. Oi! Cheeky pup. Back to work!

(*LISA goes back to interpreting.*)

Ladies and Gentlemen, our country is at war but the show must go on! So tonight, in spite of everything that's happening, we can allow ourselves some light entertainment.

(*GALYA lowers PUPPET-KATE into view.*)

(*Onstage, KATE appears, lowered from above, performing aerial.*)

(*GALYA exits.*)

(*A SOLDIER enters.*)

(*The SOLDIER sits. Lights a cigarette.*)

SOLDIER. You know, I fucking hate puppets. Always have. Even as a kid I thought they were stupid. What's the point? You can see the strings. You know they're not real. You know they're not alive. All I see is firewood.

(*Suspended like a puppet, KATE dances through the air. The SOLDIER watches.*)

I know you can hear me. We checked your ears and there's nothing wrong with any of you. You're lying. So you might as well stop pretending and listen to what I'm saying. We're here to help you. We're fighting for you. For your freedom. We're here to protect you. Your way of life is our way of life. We share the same culture, the same country. We speak the same language. We're the same, you and I. This...deaf republic. It's a disease. And we're the cure. You should be thanking me. If it wasn't for us, you'd be dead.

(**KATE** *lowers to the ground and beckons to the* **SOLDIER***. He approaches her.*)

SOLDIER. I want to read your lips.

(*Behind him,* **LISA** *lowers from above.*)

(**LISA** *strangles the* **SOLDIER***.*)

(**KATE** *stabs him.*)

(*They attach a rope around the* **SOLDIER***'s dead body and he rises up, disappearing out of sight.*)

(*They are both thrilled, brimming with adrenaline.*)

(*They sign to each other.*)

KATE. Yes! Yes! Did you see that? We were like –

(*She repeats stabbing motion.*)

LISA. Yeah yeah and he was like –

(*She enacts dying motion.*)

We got the fucker!

KATE. Yeah but you've got to be quicker next time.

LISA. Sorry.

KATE. I mean, if he'd tried anything I'd've chopped his cock off but still...

(**KATE** *sits.*)

(*Blood drips down from where the* **SOLDIER** *was raised.*)

*(**GALYA** enters with **ANUSHKA** on her arm and holding a bucket in her hand. She positions the bucket to catch the blood.)*

*(**LISA** moves over to sit with **KATE**.)*

LISA. I saw him talking to you.

KATE. Yeah, I'd say he loves the sound of his own voice.

LISA. What do you think he was saying?

KATE. Fuck knows! We don't have to listen anymore! Deaf privilege!

*(Another **SOLDIER** enters. He is played by the same actor that played the previous **SOLDIER**. They all look at him.)*

SOLDIER. Why do you look so surprised? Oh, don't tell me. We all look the same to you.

*(**SOLDIER** walks up to the bucket. Looks up.)*

Leak in the roof? Fucking state of this country. Thank god we're here. Place is falling to pieces.

*(**GALYA** points to her ear.)*

Naturally.

*(**KATE** holds out her hand. The **SOLDIER** takes it and she leads him off, through the curtains.)*

*(**GALYA** watches them go, and then turns to the audience.)*

*(**GALYA** speaks, **LISA** signs.)*

GALYA. *(To audience.)* Didn't I tell you my girls are talented? Oh yes, I put a lot of trust in them, especially this one, my extra pair of hands.

> (**GALYA** *produces a knife from behind* **ANUSHKA** *and hands it to* **LISA**.)

GALYA. *(To audience.)* What? I'd do it myself but my hands are full, as you can see. A war is one thing but a baby – wait.

What's that smell?

Ah, yes.

Parenthood costs us a little dignity.

> (**LISA** *exits in the direction of* **KATE** *and the* **SOLDIER**.)

> (**GALYA** *moves to the chair and puts* **ANUSHKA** *on the table.*)

Oh God.

> (**SONYA** *enters.*)

It's times like these I wish your mother was still around.

> (*She goes to the baby* **ANUSHKA** *and starts to change her nappy while also interpreting for* **GALYA**.)

Don't get me wrong, I'm not lazy. Far from it. It's just that between managing this theatre, looking after my girls, and...*taking care* of soldiers, it doesn't leave much time for changing filthy nappies! Ah, but you know what they say, a woman's work is never done? And the women of Vasenka are the hardest working in the world. The bravest, the strongest. And yes, the most beautiful. Beautiful are the women of Vasenka. Beautiful. In this time each of us does something for our country. Some die. Others give speeches. And now, at fifty-three, having given up all thought of having a child, here I am changing nappies! But I thank god. I thank God, Anushka, I really do.

*(**SONYA** has changed the nappy.)*

Ah, there you go! That wasn't so hard after all! I'm getting better at this.

*(**SONYA** exits.)*

*(The **SOLDIER** has been raised up out of view.)*

Right. Come on, girls. On with the show!

(The gauze lowers.)

(On it we see projected the red curtains.)

*(A **SOLDIER** enters.)*

*(**LISA** and **KATE** lead the **SOLDIER** offstage, through the curtains.)*

*(We see the offstage scene – **KATE**, **LISA**, and the **SOLDIER** – projected live onto the gauze.)*

*(As **GALYA** speaks surtitles appear on the gauze.)*

*(To **ANUSHKA**.)* Oh, Anushka.

How to say I only want some quiet; I, a deaf woman, want some quiet, I want some quiet.

*(As **GALYA** sings a nursery rhyme to **ANUSHKA**, on the gauze we see **LISA** and **KATE** strangle and stab a **SOLDIER**.)*

(The song finishes.)

*(**LISA** and **KATE** enter from behind the curtains. They are covered in blood.)*

(Spoken, captioned.) Beautiful are the women of Vasenka. Beautiful!

(The gauze rises.)

GALYA. *(Spoken, captioned.)* Clean yourself up, girls. The Sergeant's having a party later. There's a big group of them. *(To **KATE**.)* Here. Take, Anushka.

> *(**KATE** takes the baby and exits.)*

> *(**GALYA** and **LISA** sign. The dialogue is captioned.)*

LISA. That last one. He made me choke. His hands. In my hair. I told him to stop. I signed *be good*. I knew he wouldn't understand. I signed again. Be good. I can still feel his hands. Holding my hair like strings.

GALYA. It'll be over soon.

LISA. When?

GALYA. When they're all dead.

LISA. There's always another soldier. And another. And another. They don't care about their men. They outnumber us. We can't win. It'll never end.

GALYA. There'll be an ending.

LISA. No. We'll be doing this forever. It's already been two years. This scene has happened over and over again. Exactly the same. You sat there. And I stood here. This has all happened before. But now it's two years later.

> *(**LISA** exits.)*

> *(A young girl walks in. She is about two years old. She is a puppet. This is **ANUSHKA**.)*

> *(**ANUSHKA** is being puppeteered by **SONYA** and **ALFONSO**.)*

GALYA. *(Spoken, captioned.)* Anushka! What are you doing here! I only left you for a moment.

*(**ANUSHKA** wobbles towards **GALYA**.)*

Wow! Wow! Look at you. Turning into a little adventurer! Oh, Anushka. So grown up! You're nearly a real person! Come here to me. Sit. I've got something to show you.

*(**ANUSHKA** moves towards **GALYA**.)*

*(**GALYA** gets the **PUPPET-ALFONSO** and walks it over to **ANUSHKA**.)*

You know who this is? Do you recognise him? It's your daddy.

He was very brave man. That's where you get it from.

Such defiance.

(Pretending to be the puppet speaking.)

I look at you, Anushka,
and say

to the late caterpillars

goodmorning, Senators!
This is a battle

worthy
of our weapons!

(Her voice again.) What do you think? No? Fair enough. I guess you're a bit grown up for puppets.

*(She puts the puppet away and sits down opposite **ANUSHKA**.)*

Oh, Anushka. If only your parents could see you now. To see who you're becoming.

Ah, but they can.

I know they can.

They're always with you.

After all, it was them that made you.

Remember that any time you feel alone.

> (**ALFONSO** *and* **SONYA** *let go of* **ANUSHKA** *and exit.*)

Now.

To bed, Anushka!

Into your pyjamas.

> (**GALYA** *picks* **ANUSHKA** *up.*)

Anushka, your pyjamas –
they are the final meanings of my life.

To get you into your pyjamas,
Anushka!

So much to live for.

> (*The* **SOLDIER** *enters.*)

SOLDIER. You must be Galya. I've heard so much about this place from the other soldiers. To be honest with you, I'm quite picky when it comes to theatre. If I see something I don't like it can put me in a really bad mood.

> (**GALYA** *hesitates, then points to her ear.*)

Of course. Silly me.

> (**GALYA** *exits.*)

Seriously, though, I've heard it's a great show.

Excellent reviews.

Don't get me wrong. I still hate puppets.

But I have to admit, I'm starting to see the appeal.

*(The **SOLDIER** moves behind the puppet theatre.)*

You can have the world the way you want it.

And people the way you want them.

*(He lowers the **PUPPET-KATE** into the puppet theatre.)*

(She lowers from above, but upside down.)

You can do whatever you want.

*(The **SOLDIER** moves the car into the puppet theatre. The car appears on stage.)*

And you can make anything happen.

*(The **SOLDIER** sprinkles snow in the puppet theatre.)*

(It starts to snow on stage.)

The only limit is your imagination.

*(The **SOLDIER** approaches **KATE**.)*

Don't worry.

I'm not going to kill you.

I just want to talk.

That's all I've ever wanted.

It's not my fault you won't listen.

That's the thing with you made up countries.

Puppet states.

You don't know what's good for you.

You think you can exist without us. But you're wrong.

We're pulling the strings.

And in the end, you'll thank us.

Because, even though no one will admit it, the truth is, people want to be manipulated.

It's human nature!

> *(The* **SOLDIER** *opens the door and drags* **PAVEL** *out.)*

I don't know what you're hoping to see.

But if it's evidence you want.

Now's your chance.

> *(The* **SOLDIER** *holds the gun up to* **PAVEL**.*)*

Shoot.

> *(The gauze lowers.)*

> *(Panicked,* **PAVEL** *turns the camera on and* **KATE** *appears on the gauze.)*

> *(The* **SOLDIER** *then opens the bonnet of the car. He runs cables from the car battery and holds them near* **KATE**.*)*

For what you did to soldier Ivanoff.

> *(He presses the cables against her.)*

For what you did to soldier Petrovich.

> *(He presses the cables against her again.)*

For what you did to soldier Debenko.

> *(He presses the cables against her again.)*

You can make it stop. All you have to do is admit you can hear me.

*(**KATE** starts signing.)*

What are you saying?

*(The **SOLDIER** points his gun at **PAVEL**.)*

What the fuck is she saying?

*(**KATE** signs, **PAVEL** speaks. The text appears captioned on the gauze.)*

KATE. *(Signs.)* Forgive me, I
was not honest with you,
life –
to you I stand answerable.
Whoever listens:
thank you for the feather on my tongue,
thank you for our argument that ends, thank you for deafness,
Lord, such fire
from a match you never lit.

SOLDIER. What the fuck does that mean?

PAVEL. I think it's a poem.

SOLDIER. Nonsense.

*(The **SOLDIER** shoots **PAVEL**.)*

You people need to learn to speak properly.

*(**GALYA** enters.)*

It's over. Whatever it was. This little show of yours. Your little rebellion. It was never going to work. You've just made things worse for yourself. You see, soldiers don't like looking foolish. Besides, I'm sure by now you've realised: you'll never kill me, just men who look like me.

*(The **SOLDIER** exits.)*

(Gauze rises.)

(GALYA *moves to* **KATE** *and she lowers to the ground.)*

(GALYA *kneels next to her.)*

(LISA *is there.)*

(GALYA *notices her.)*

GALYA. Yes, yes, you – come. Come!

> **(GALYA** *scrambles towards the audience.* **LISA** *stays behind her.)*

Don't worry, citizens.

It's not over.

We can still fight!

Deafness rests in our men's chests! Remember!?

We have our bodies, and as long as we have our bodies, we can fight!

It's not over!

It's not over!

> **(LISA** *stops signing and stands, exhausted.)*

It's not over!!

> **(GALYA** *turns to look at* **LISA**.)

It's not over! I said: it's not over!!

LISA. *(Signs.)* It is over. It's finished. We can't fight anymore.

GALYA. *(Unsigned.)* What are you saying? Why are you saying that??

> **(GALYA** *walks forward and looks up at the caption screen, her back to the audience.)*

LISA. Tonight they shot fifty women on Lerna Street. They arrested every woman on Tedna Street. They say they'll bomb a new store every day for what Galya's girls did to soldier Ivanoff. For what Galya's girls did to soldier Petrovich. For what Galya's girls did to soldier Debenko.

GALYA. *(Signed.)* The things you did!

LISA. *(Signed.)* The things you made us do.

GALYA. *(Signed.)* You're not a puppet.

LISA. *(Signed.)* I was a child.

GALYA. *(Spoken.)* A child learns the world by putting it in her mouth, a girl becomes a woman and a woman, earth.

> *(**LISA** spits in her face.)*

LISA. *(Signed.)* I'm not doing this anymore. Interpreting. *Your* work. You have hands. Use them.

> *(**LISA** exits.)*

> *(Suddenly a deep bass sound moves through the theatre.)*

> *(As **GALYA** speaks, theatre lights fall all around her.)*

GALYA. *(Spoken, captioned.)* Go home! All of you!

You heard what she said.

It's over.

You!

You haven't kissed your wife since Noah was a sailor!

What's wrong with you all!

Go!

Too many ears and no one attached to them.

Marvellous cretins!

I taught you all!

I taught you that

Deafness isn't an illness! It's a sexual position!

I taught you how to speak to homeless dogs as if they
are men,
speak to men

as if they are men
and not just souls on crutches of bone

My dear neighbours! Marvellous cretins!

> (*The bombing continues.* **GALYA** *goes and
> rescues* **PUPPET-GALYA**.)

My little theatre.

Who would bomb a theatre?

What's the point in that?

It's only a play.

> (**LISA** *enters with a woodchipper.*)

(*Spoken.*) I see how it is. You won't take my knife but
you'll stab me in the back.

> (**KATE** *and* **PAVEL** *stand up. They go to the
> woodchipper and turn it on. It roars.*)

> (*They go to the puppet theatre and
> collect* **PUPPET-GALYA** *and move it to the
> woodchipper.*)

(*Spoken.*) Dig a good hole!
Lay me nostrils up

and shovel in my mouth the decent black earth.

*(**GALYA** exits.)*

*(**LISA** and **KATE** feed the **PUPPET-GALYA** into the woodchipper spraying sawdust across the stage.)*

(They exit.)

(Pause.)

*(**SONYA** and **ALFONSO** enter.)*

*(**ALFONSO** is in the middle of the stage, as at the start. **SONYA** to the side, as at the start.)*

*(**ALFONSO** signs, **SONYA** speaks.)*

ALFONSO. *(Signed.)* Our country has surrendered.

Years later, some will say none of this happened: the shops were open, we were happy and went to see puppet shows in the town square.

We'd sit in the audience, silently, like none of this happened.

And in a way, it's true, none of this *did* happen.

I made it up.

Because of course my name isn't Alfonso, and her name isn't Sonya.

And you are not the townspeople of Vasenka.

It was just a story.

I tried to tell a story.

After all, that's why we go to the theatre.

To try and understand each other.

To understand the world.

But sometimes it doesn't work.

Sometimes however hard we try

it remains inaccessible.

And when it's over

we leave the theatre

and say thank God.

it didn't happen to me.

it didn't happen to us.

We lived happily during the War

And when they bombed other people's houses, we

protested
but not enough, we opposed them but not

enough. I was
in my bed, around my bed the world

was falling: invisible house by invisible house by
invisible house –

I took a chair outside and watched the sun

in the street of money in the city of money in the
country of money,

our great country of money, we (forgive us)

lived happily during the war.

> *(Wires lower: wires for* **ALFONSO** *and wires
> for* **SONYA**.*)*

> *(They attach each other and slowly rise up.)*

> *(As they rise from the floor their bodies go
> limp, dead.)*

(As they rise, all the other **PEOPLE** *from over the course of the evening are lowered from above. They hang suspended in the space.)*

(Silence.)

(The **SOLDIER** *walks through the hanging maze of people. He moves to the front and addresses the audience.)*

(He signs for the first time.)

SOLDIER. *(Captioned.)* There's an old joke.

A man is sent away to a prison camp and tells his friend he'll write to him when he gets there to tell him what it's like.

He says if things are good, he'll write the letter in blue ink.

And if things are bad, he'll write in red ink.

Some months later, the friend receives a letter.

It's in blue ink.

It says:

Hey! Things are actually great here! People are really friendly, the weather's fantastic and you can do whatever you want. You can go to the theatre, you can go to the pub, all the shops are open. In fact, you can get anything you want…

Except for red ink.

(Blackout.)

9 780573 000881